Learn French

A Guide to Learning the Basics of a New Language

By Jenna Swan

Table of Contents

Why Learn French?

Fluency in any language other than your native tongue can open up a lot of opportunities for you, but if absolute fluency is not possible, then a better understanding of the language is almost as beneficial. French is a popular choice among native English speakers because understanding it helps them communicate better when visiting France, Canada, Switzerland, Belgium, and other countries which use French as an official language. Although many of the locals in these countries can also understand and speak English, they get a sense of pride from knowing that foreign visitors took the time and effort to learn *their* language. Communicating with these people becomes easier since you no longer have to figure out what they're trying to say (and vice-versa). The same goes for those French words you'll come across on street signs, newspapers, maps, etc.

It may not be evident at first, but a better understanding of French will ensure that you have more time exploring and enjoying the best that the country has to offer: tourist attractions, arts and entertainment activities, and the local cuisine to name a few (and French-speaking countries are often highly known for such). But what if you are due to travel anytime soon? Is it still possible to master at least the basics of the French language if you're given only a week to do so? Fortunately, it is possible, and this book will help you do just that.

This book features not only basic French grammar rules but also easy-to-understand guides on how the language can best be used in various situations.

And the best part is, with the help of this book, you will learn to master all that and more!

Chapter 1: Pronunciation Guide

The French Alphabet

French and English share a similar alphabet consisting of 26 letters but have different pronunciation for many of the letters. In addition, French makes use of accents on vowels which make each vowel sound distinct.

Aa [ɑ]	Bb [be]	Cc [se]
Dd [de]	Ee [ə]	Ff [ɛf]
Gg [ʒe]	Hh [aʃ]	Ii [i]
Jj [ʒi]	Kk [ka]	Ll [ɛl]
Mm [ɛm]	Nn [ɛn]	Oo [o]
Pp [pe]	Qq [ky]	Rr [ɛʀ]
Ss [ɛs]	Tt [te]	Uu [y]
Vv [ve]	Ww [dubləve]	Xx [iks]
Y y [igʀɛk]	Zz [zɛd]	

Consonants		Example
c	before e or i, sounds like 's'	ceci
c	elsewhere, it sounds like 'k'	car
ç	sounds like 's'	ça
ch	sounds like 'sh'	château
g	before e or i, sounds like 's' in 'measure'	général
g	elsewhere, sounds like 'g' in 'go'	gare
h	is silent	hôtel
j	like 's' in 'measure'	je
qu, q	sound like 'k'	qui
r	pronounced at the back of the throat	rire
s	at the beginning of a word it is a 's' sound at the back of the throat	salle

| s | between two vowels, it makes a 'z' sound | rose |

Chapter 2: Liaisons and Elision

Liaisons

Liaisons are partly to blame for the difficulty in French pronunciation and aural cognition. A liaison refers to the linking of a latently-silent consonant at the end of one word to the beginning of the following word which results in the pronunciation of the consonant.

In French, except for "l" and "f", all consonants placed at the end of a word are not pronounced. However, when a word that ends with a consonant is followed by a word that begins with a vowel or the mute h, the consonant is pronounced at the start of the word that follows.

For example:

vous [vu]	vous avez [vu za vay]
un [uh(n)]	un homme [uh(n) nuhm]
les [lay]	les amis [lay za mee]
ont [o(n)]	ont-ils [o(n) teel]
trois [twah]	trois amis [twa za mee]
chez [shay]	chez eux [shez urh]

Consonants in liaisons may also change in pronunciation. An "s", for instance, is pronounced like a "z" in a liaison.

Not all liaisons, however, have to be pronounced. In certain cases, liaison may be possible but pronunciation is optional.

For example:

les étudiants et les jeunes

les larmes et les cris

Elision

In elision, the opposite of liaison happens. Sounds that are usually pronounced become silent. The vowel sounds of the following one-syllable words go silent when placed before a vowel or mute h:

je, me, te, se, le, la, de, ne, que, jusque

French orthography marks elision by replacing the vowel with an apostrophe and combining the words.

j'ai
il t'aime
l'enfant
l'amour

Chapter 3: Greetings and Salutations

Learning how to greet people and start polite conversations is an essential aspect of learning a new language.

The basic French greeting "bonjour" [bohn-jhoor] is used to say good morning, good afternoon, or hello. In the evening, you say "bonsoir" [bohn-swahr].

Here are other useful greetings and polite expressions that you can use in a French-speaking country. Use them freely and appropriately in your interactions.

French	Pronunciation	English
bienvenue	[bee-ehn veh-noo]	welcome
enchanté (to males)	[ahn-shant-ay]	pleased to meet you
enchantée (to females)	[ahn-shant-ay]	pleased to meet you
S'il vous plaît	[seel vooh pleh]	please
merci	[mehr-see]	thank you
merci beaucoup	[mehr-see bo-koo]	thank you very much
Je vous en prie	[zhuh vooh-zahN pree]	you're welcome
De rien	[duh ryahN]	you're welcome
salut	[sah-loo]	hello or goodbye
à bientôt	[ah bee-ehn-toe]	see you soon
à demain	[ah deh-mehn]	see you tomorrow
à toute à l'heure	[ah toot ah luhr]	see you later
adieu	[ah-dyuh]	goodbye
au revoir	[oh reh-vwah]	goodbye
bonne chance	[bohn shahnce]	good luck
bonne nuit	[bohn nwee]	goodnight
santé	[sahn-tay]	cheers
pardon	[pahr-dohN]	excuse me
excusez-moi	[eks-kew-zey-mwah]	excuse me

Chapter 4: Introductions

Very often, you'll come across situations where you have to introduce yourself or somebody. First impressions last so you have to know how to present yourself properly.

It's common courtesy to start the introduction with a greeting before proceeding to introduce yourself.

Bonjour, Je m'appelle _(Name)_	Good day, my name is _____
Bonjour, Je suis _(Name)_	Good day, I'm _____

To introduce a companion, your wife for instance, you'll say:

Je vous présente Arianne, ma femme.	Let me introduce you my wife, Arianne.

If you're introducing a friend:

Voici Jean Pierre, mon ami.	This is my friend, Jean Pierre.

When addressing someone you're meeting for the first time, it's polite to use the "vous" form to convey formality. The "tu" form is more appropriate when speaking to children.

Comment vous appelez-vous? (Formal)	What's your name?
Comment t'appelles-tu? (Informal)	What's your name?

When they reply and give their name, you're expected to acknowledge the introduction and express your pleasure at meeting them with these phrases:

C'est un plaisir de vous rencontrer.	It's a pleasure to meet you.
Enchanté de faire votre connaissance	Delighted to make your acquaintance.

Enchanté.	Delighted.

You can reply to an introduction with this phrase:

Moi de meme.	[mwah dmehm]	The pleasure is mine.

You could also talk about where you're from or your age.

J'habite à New York.	I live in New York.
J'ai 32 ans.	I am 32.

You can also ask them about their country of origin:

De quel pays êtes-vous?	What country are you from?

Chapter 5: Nouns (Noms)

A noun represents a person, place, thing, or idea. In French, nouns are either masculine or feminine. Learning a noun's gender along with the noun itself is important because articles and adjectives as well as some pronouns and verbs have to agree with the nouns they modify.

The best approach to learning nouns and their gender is by learning the noun with the appropriate definite or indefinite article.

Examples:

une banane	feminine	a banana
un citron	masculine	a lemon
une tasse	feminine	a cup
un poisson	masculine	a fish
la nuit	feminine	the night
la journée	feminine	the day / daytime
le soleil	masculine	the sun
la lune	feminine	the moon
la voiture	feminine	the car
le camion	masculine	the truck
la chaussure	feminine	the shoe
le sac	masculine	the bag
la terre	feminine	the earth
le moteur	masculine	the engine

When nouns define persons, the gender normally corresponds to the gender of the person.

Examples:

un homme	masculine
une femme	feminine

Forming plural nouns

In general, French nouns change to plural by adding –s at the end. Though written, the –s is mute and plurality in speech is recognized by modifiers or indicators such as articles or pronouns.

Examples:

Singular	Plural	English
l'ami	les amis	friend(s)
le clou	les clous	nail(s)
la mère	les mères	mother(s)
mon ami	mes amis	my friend(s)
ce clou	ces clous	this nail, these nails
ma mère	nos mères	my mother, our mothers

Below are exceptions to the general rule:

Nouns ending in –s, -x, -z don't change.

le tas	les tas	heap
la croix	les croix	cross
le nez	les nez	nose

Nouns ending -au, -eau, -eu form their plural by adding –x.

le tuyau	les tuyaux	drainpipe
le neveu	les neveux	nephew
le gâteau	les gâteaux	cake

Exception:

| le pneu | les pneus | tyre |
| le bleu | les bleus | bruise |

French nouns ending in –al change to –aux in plural form

Singular   Plural

le corail	les coraux	coral
l'émail	les émaux	enamel
le travail	les travaux	work
le vitrail	les vitraux	stained glass window

Nouns endings -ou change to plural by adding -x

Singular	Plural	English
le bijou	les bijoux	jewel
le genou	les genoux	knee
le hibou	les hiboux	owl

le pou	les poux	louse
le caillou	les cailloux	pebble
le chou	les choux	cabbage
le joujou	les joujoux	toy

Irregular plural forms

Singular	Plural	English
l'aïeul	les aïeux	ancestor
le bonhomme	les bonshommes	fellow
le ciel	les cieux	sky
l'oeil	les yeux	eye
Madame	Mesdames	Mrs
Mademoiselle	Mesdemoiselles	Miss
Monsieur	Messieurs	Mr

To form the plural of most family names, a noun modifier signifying plurality is used instead of adding –s to the family name.

Example: les Dupont   the Duponts

For illustrious family names, however, the plurals are formed by adding –s and using the appropriate article:

Examples:

les Stuarts	the Stuarts
les Bourbons	the Bourbons
les Plantagenets	the Plantagenets

Pluralia Tantum

Some nouns are used only in the plural form:

Examples:

agissements (m)	actions
annales (f)	annals
appointements (m)	royalty
archives (f)	archive
besicles (f)	spectacles
bestiaux (m)	beasts
broussailles (f)	bushes
confins (m)	boundaries
décombres (f)	debris
ébats (m)	game
entrailles(f)	intestines
funérailles (f)	funeral
honoraires (m)	honorarium
mânes (m)	ghosts
mœurs (f)	customs
pierreries (f)	jewels
ténèbres (f)	darkness
vêpres (f)	vesper
vivres (m)	victuals

Singularia Tantum

There are nouns that are used only in the singular such as the following categories:

Nouns that designate phenomena and objects unique in themselves:

la lune	moon
le soleil	sun
le nord	north
le sud	south
l'horizon	horizon

Nouns that designate materials, substances, or products:

le charbon	coal
le lait	milk
le blé	wheat

Abstract nouns that denote quality, state, or action:

la joie	joy
le développement	development
l'orgueil	proud
la vaillance	valor

Nouns that imply total plurality:

l'argent	money
le pavage	pavement

The names of the sciences and nouns ending in –isme:

l'impressionisme	impressionism
la médicine	medical science
la biologie	biology

Masculine Nouns

le père	[luh pehr]	father
le grand-père	[luh grahN-pehr]	grandfather
le garçon	[luh gahr-sohN]	boy
l'ami	[lah-mee]	friend (m.)
un homme	[uhN nohm]	man
un oncle	[uhN nohN-kluh]	uncle
un cousin	[uhN koo-zaN]	cousin (m.)
un ami	[uhN nah-mee]	friend (m.)

Feminine Nouns

la mère	[lah mehr]	mother
la grand-mère	[lah grahN-mehr]	grandmother
la fille	[la fee-y]	girl
l'amie	[lah-mee]	friend (f.)
une femme	[ewn fahm]	woman
une tante	[ewn tahNt]	aunt
une cousine	[ewn koo-zeen]	cousin (f.)
une amie	[ewn nah-mee]	friend (f.)

Chapter 6: Determiners (Déterminants)

Determiners are words that introduce or modify a noun. Articles and specific types of adjectives function as determiners and they always agree in number and gender with the noun they refer to.

Articles

The most common markers in French are definite articles that express "the" and indefinite articles that express "a", "an", "one", or "some".

Articles

	Definite	Indefinite	Partitive
masculine, singular	le	un	du
feminine, singular	la	une	de la
before a vowel	l'	un/une	de l'
plural	les	des	des

Definite articles refer to a specific noun:

Example:

l'ami	the friend
l'oignon	the onion

Indefinite articles denote an unspecified noun:

Example:

une pomme	an apple
un ami	a friend

Partitive article correspond to "some" and "any" in English and indicate an unknown quantity.

Example:

de l'oignon	some onions
des pommes	some apples

Adjectives

Demonstrative adjectives (Adjectifs Démonstratifs)

Demonstrative adjectives refer to a specific noun.

	Singular	English	Plural	English
Masculine	ce, cet	this	ces	these
Feminine	cette	this	ces	these

The masculine demonstrative adjective "ce" becomes "cet" when it is placed before a noun which starts in a vowel or silent h.

Examples:

Singular		Plural	
cet oignon	this onion	ces oignons	these onions
cette fleur	this flower	ces fleurs	these flowers
ce garçon	this boy	ces garcons	these boys
cet arbre	this tree	ces arbres	these trees

Possessive Adjectives (Adjectifs Possessifs)

Possessive adjectives, also called possessive determiners, show ownership and must agree with the number and gender of the noun they modify.

Singular	Singular	Singular	Plural	English
mon	ma	mon	mes	my
ton	ta	ton	tes	your ("tu" form)
son	sa	son	ses	his, her, its
notre	notre	notre	nos	our
votre	votre	votre	vos	your ("vous" form)
leur	leur	leur	leurs	their

Examples:

ma mere	my mother
mon père	my father
mon amie	my female friend
ton stylo	your pen
tes livres	your books
notre père	our father
notre mère	our mother
son amie	his, her, its female friend
ses livres	his, her, its book
leur stylo	their pen
leurs montres	their watches

When referring to two or more nouns, a possessive adjective is placed before each noun.

Example:

mon oncle et ma tante	my uncle and my aunt
sa sœur et son frère	his sister and brother

Interrogative Adjectives (Adjectifs Interrogatifs)

Interrogative adjectives are used to clarify which among two or more nouns is being referred to. The interrogative adjective "quel" means "which" or "what" and it has four forms.

	Singular	Plural
Masculine	quel	quels
Feminine	quelle	quelles

Quel temps fait-il?	What's the weather like?
Quel jour sommes-nous?	What day is it?
Quelle heure est-il?	What time is it?
Quels fruits aimez-vous?	Which fruits do you like?
Quels cours vas-tu prendre?	Which classes will you take?
Quelles pommes aime-t-il?	Which apples does he like?
Quelles sont tes couleurs préférées?	What are your favorite colors?

Indefinite Adjectives (Adjectifs Indéfinis)

Indefinite adjectives are words used to describe nouns in an unspecific sense.

French indefinite adjectives

autre(s)	other
certain(e)(s)	certain
chaque	each
divers(es)	various
maint(e)(s)	many
plusieurs	several
quelque(s)	some, a few
tel	some, any
tout(e)(s)	all, every

Examples:

Ça c'est autre chose.	That's another story.
Elle a un certain sourire.	She has a certain smile.
Chaque étudiant doit parler.	Each student must speak.
Il a quelques livres à lire.	He has a few books to read.
Il a plusieurs amis.	He has several friends.
Ils ont tout compris.	They understood everything.

Numerical Adjectives

While all numbers are numerical adjectives, only cardinal numbers are classified as determiners.

Elle a deux voitures.	She has two cars.
J'ai trois livres.	I have three books.

Exclamative Adjectives (Adjectifs exclamatifs)

"Quel", a French exclamative adjective, is placed before a noun to express astonishment, admiration, indignation, or other strong emotions about that noun.

	Singular	Plural
Masculine	quel	quels
Feminine	quelle	quelles

Quel génie!	What a genius!
Quelle catastrophe!	What a catastrophe!
Quelle horreur!	How horrible!
Quels imbéciles!	What fools!
Quelles bonnes idées!	What good ideas!

Negative Adjectives (Adjectifs negatives)

Negative adjectives are used to negate, refuse, or cast doubt on a quality of a noun. Like negative pronouns and negative adverbs, they have two parts that are placed around the verb.

Negative adjectives	English
ne... aucun(e)	no, not any
ne... nul(le)	no, not any
ne... pas un(e)	no, not one
ne... pas un(e) seul(e)	not a single

Examples:

Je ne connais aucun avocet.	I don't know any lawyers.
Aucun argent n'a été retrouvé.	No money was found.

Chapter 7: Numbers

Learning how to count in French is quite simple. They key is to learn the first one hundred numbers and after that, all you have to do is to place the hundreds before numbers 1 to 99.

For example:

101	cent un	[son uh]
102	cent deux	[son duhr]
203	deux cent trois	[duhr son twa]
305	trois cent cinq	[trois son sank]

Facile, non? (Easy, right?)

In writing numbers, French uses a comma in place of a period in English and uses a period where English uses a comma.

For instance:

English	1,265,132.25
French	1.265.132,25

A comma is translated to "virgule" in French. Hence, deux virgule vingt-cinq is 2,25 in French and 2.25 in English.

Hyphens are only used on numbers below 100.

0	zéro	[zay-ro]
1	un	[uh]
2	deux	[duhr]
3	trois	[twa]
4	quatre	[katr]

5	cinq	[sank]
6	six	[sees]
7	sept	[set]
8	huit	[weet]
9	neuf	[nurf]
10	dix	[dees]
11	onze	[onz]
12	douze	[dooz]
13	treize	[trez]
14	quatorze	[katorz]
15	quinze	[kanz]
16	seize	[sez]
17	dix-sept	[dee-set]
18	dix-huit	[dees-weet]
19	dix-neuf	[dees-nurf]
20	vingt	[van]
21	vingt et un	[vant-ay-uh]
22	vingt-deux	[van-duhr]
23	vingt-trois	[van-twa]
24	vingt-quatre	[van-katr]
25	vingt-cinq	[van-sank]
26	vingt-six	[van-sees]
27	vingt-sept	[van-set]
28	vingt-huit	[van-weet]
29	vingt-neuf	[van-nurf]
30	trente	[tront]
31	trente et un	[tront ay-uh]
32	trente-deux	[tront-durh]
33	trente-trois	[tront-twa]
34	trente-quatre	[tront-katr]

35	trente-cinq	[tront-sank]
36	trente-six	[tront-sees]
37	trente-sept	[tront-set]
38	trente-huit	[tront-weet]
39	trente-neuf	[tront-nurf]
40	quarante	[karont]
41	quarante et un	[karont-ay-uh]
42	quarante-deux	[karont-deux]
43	quarante-trois	[karont-twa]
44	quarante-quatre	[karont-katr]
45	quarante-cinq	[karont-sank]
46	quarante-six	[karont-sees]
47	quarante-sept	[karont-set]
48	quarante-huit	[karont-weet]
49	quarante-neuf	[karont-nurf]
50	cinquante	[sank-ont]
51	cinquante et un	[sank-ont-ay-uh]
52	cinquante-deux	[sank-ont-deux]
53	cinquante-trois	[sank-ont-twa]
54	cinquante-quatre	[sank-ont-katr]
55	cinquante-cinq	[sank-ont-sank]
56	cinquante-six	[sank-ont-sees]
57	cinquante-sept	[sank-ont-set]
58	cinquante-huit	[sank-ont-weet]
59	cinquante-neuf	[sank-ont-nurf]
60	soixante	[swa-sont]
61	soixante et un	[swa-sont-ay-un]
62	soixante-deux	[swa-sont-dur]
63	soixante-trois	[swa-sont-twa]
64	soixante-quatre	[swa-sont-katr]

65	soixante-cinq	[swa-sont-sank]
66	soixante-six	[swa-sont-sees]
67	soixante-sept	[swa-sont-set]
68	soixante-huit	[swa-sont-weet]
69	soixante-neuf	[swa-sont-nurf]
70	soixante-dix	[swa-sont-dees]
71	soixante-et-onze	[swa-sont-ay-onz]
72	soixante-douze	[swa-sont-dooz]
73	soixante-treize	[swa-sont-trez]
74	soixante-quatorze	[swa-sont-katorz]
75	soixante-quinze	[swa-sont-kanz]
76	soixante-seize	[swa-sont-sez]
77	soixante-dix-sept	[swa-sont-dee-set]
78	soixante-dix-huit	[swa-sont-dees-weet]
79	soixante-dix-neuf	[swa-sont-dees-nurf]
80	quatre-vingts	[kat-ra-van]
81	quatre-vingt-un	[kat-ra-vant-uh]
82	quatre-vingt-deux	[kat-ra-van-dur]
83	quatre-vingt-trois	[kat-ra-van-twa]
84	quatre-vingt-quatre	[kat-ra-van-katr]
85	quatre-vingt-cinq	[kat-ra-van-sank]
86	quatre-vingt-six	[kat-ra-van-sees]
87	quatre-vingt-sept	[kat-ra-van-set]
88	quatre-vingt-huit	[kat-ra-van-weet]
89	quatre-vingt-neuf	[kat-ra-van-nurf]
90	quatre-vingt-dix	[kat-ra-van-dees]
91	quatre-vingt-onze	[kat-ra-van-onz]
92	quatre-vingt-douze	[kat-ra-van-dooz]
93	quatre-vingt-treize	[kat-ra-van- trez]
94	quatre-vingt-quatorze	[kat-ra-van-katorz]

95	quatre-vingt-quinze	[kat-ra-van- kanz]
96	quatre-vingt-seize	[kat-ra-van- sez]
97	quatre-vingt-dix-sept	[kat-ra-van- dee-set]
98	quatre-vingt-dix-huit	[kat-ra-van- dees-weet]
99	quatre-vingt-dix-neuf	[kat-ra-van- dees-nurf]
100	cent	[son]
200	deux cent	[duhr son]
300	trois cent	[twa son]
400	quatre cent	[katr son]
500	cinq cent	[sank son]
600	six cent	[sees son]
700	sept cent	[set son]
800	huit cent	[weet son]
900	neuf cent	[nurf son]
1000	mille	[meel]
2000	deux mille	[dew meel]
2.000.000	un million	[oon mee-lee-on]
3.000.000	deux millions	[duhr mee-lee-ons]
1.000.000.000	un milliard	[oon mee-lee-ar]

Chapter 8: Time

| Quelle heure est-il? | [kehl uhr eh-teel?] | What time is it? |

It's quite easy to tell time in French if you are familiar with numbers.

To express time after the hour, you simply add the minutes. To express time before the hour, use "moins" which is equivalent to before, less, or minus. "Et" is used only with "quart" et "demi(e)".

To express half past midnight/noon, use Il est minuit/midi et demi. To express half past for all other hours, use the hour and then "et demi(e)."

Il est une heure.	[eel eh tewn nuhr]	It is 1:00.
Il est quatre heures et quart.	[eel eh kahtr uhr ay kahr]	It is 4:15.
Il est six heures vingt-cinq.	[eel eh see zuhr vaN-saNk]	It is 6:25.
Il est onze heures moins dix.	[eel eh ohN zuhr mwaN dees]	It is 10:50.
Il est midi moins cinq.	[eel eh mee-dee mwaN saNk]	It is 11:55.
Il est deux heures cinq.	[eel eh duh zuhr saNk]	It is 2:05.
Il est trois heures dix.	[eel eh trwah zuhr dees]	It is 3:10.
Il est cinq heures vingt.	[eel eh saN kuhr vaN]	It is 5:20.
Il est sept heures et demie.	[eel eh seh tuhr ay duh-mee]	It is 7:30.
Il est minuit.	[eel eh mee-nwee]	It's midnight.

Time Expressions:

une seconde	[ewn suh-gohNd]	a second
une minute	[ewn mee-newt]	a minute
une heure	[ewn nuhr]	an hour
à quelle heure?	[ah kehl uhr]	at what time?
à une heure précise	[ah ewn uhr pray-seez]	at exactly 1:00
à deux heures précises	[ah duh zuhr pray-seez]	at exactly 2:00
à minuit précis	[ah mee-nwee pray-see]	at exactly midnight
par heure	[pahr uhr]	per hour
il y a une heure	[eel yah ewn nuhr]	an hour ago
du matin	[dew mah-taN]	in the morning (a.m.)
de l'après-midi	[lah-preh mee-dee]	in the afternoon (p.m.)
du soir	[dew swahr]	in the evening (p.m.)
un quart d'heure	[uhN kahr duhr]	a quarter of an hour
dans une heure	[dahN zew nuhr]	in an hour
avant trois heures	[ah-vahN trwah zuhr]	before 3:00
après trois heures	[ah-preh trwah zuhr]	after 3:00
en retard	[ahN ruh-tahr]	late (in arriving)
une demi-heure	[ewn duh-mee uhr]	a half hour
jusqu'à deux heures	[zhew-skah duh zuhr]	until 2:00
depuis quelle heure?	[duh-pwee see zuhr]	from what time?
depuis six heures	[duh-pwee see zuhr]	since 6:00
tard	[tahr]	late
dans	[dahN]	in
il ya	[eel yah]	ago
par	[pahr]	per
pendant	[pahN-dahN]	during
prochain(e)	[proh-shahN.proh-shehn]	next
dernier, dernière	[dehr-nyah,dehr-nyehr]	last

passé(e)	[pah-say]	last
la veille	[la vehy]	eve
avant-hier	[ah-vahN yehr]	day before yesterday
hier	[yehr]	yesterday
aujourd'hui	[oh-zhoor-dwee]	today
demain	[duh-maN]	tomorrow
après-demain	[ah-preh duh-maN]	day after tomorrow
le lendemain	[luh lahN-duh-maN]	next day
dès	[deh]	from

Chapter 9: Days of the Week

Except when they are used at the start of a sentence, the days of the week are not capitalized. Days are considered masculine.

lundi	[luhN-dee]	Monday
mardi	[mahr-dee]	Tuesday
mercredi	[ehr-kruh-dee]	Wednesday
jeudi	[zhuh-dee]	Thursday
vendredi	[vahN-druh-dee]	Friday
samedi	[sahm-dee]	Saturday
dimanche	[dee-mahNsh]	Sunday

When talking about a specific day, the article "de" is used in the same way "on" is used in English.

For example:

Le vendredi, je vais en ville.	(luh vahN-druh-dee zhuh veh zahN veel)	On Fridays, I go downtown.

Chapter 10: Months of the Year

Just like the days of the week, months are all masculine and not capitalized except when used at the beginning of a sentence.

The preposition "en" is used to indicate that an event will transpire in a specific month. For example:

Je vais en France en mai.	[zhuh veh zahN frahNs ahN meh]	I am going to France in May.

janvier	[zhahN-vyay]	January
février	[fay-vree-yay]	February
mars	[mahrs]	March
avril	[ah-vreel]	April
mai	[meh]	May
juin	[zhwaN]	June
juillet	[zhwee-eh]	July
août	[oo(t)]	August
septembre	[sehp-tahNbr]	September
octobre	[ohk-tohbr]	October
novembre	[noh-vahNbr]	November
décembre	[day-sahNbr]	December

Chapter 11: Seasons

The English preposition in is expressed in seasons with the use of either "au" for spring or "en" for winter summer, and fall.

Example:

Je vais en France en été.	[zhuh veh zahN frahNs ahN nay-tay]	I'm going to France in the summer.
Je vais en France au printemps.	[zhuh veh zahN frahNs o praN-tahN]	I'm going to France in the spring.

l'hiver	[lee-vehr]	winter
le printemps	[luh praN-tahN]	spring
l'été	[lay-tay]	summer
l'automne	[lo-tohn]	autumn, fall

Chapter 12: Pronouns (Pronoms)

Pronouns are words that replace nouns. The different kinds of pronouns may be grouped into two main categories: personal pronouns and impersonal pronouns.

Personal Pronouns

Personal pronouns are pronouns that refer to specific person, place, or thing.

There are five different kinds of personal pronouns:
1. Subject pronouns
2. Object pronouns
3. Indirect object pronouns
4. Reflexive pronoun
5. Disjunctive pronouns

Subject pronouns (Les Pronoms Soumis)

Subject pronouns are used in place of the subject or the 'doer' of the action of the verb.

Singular

First person	je	I
Second person	tu	you
Third person	il	he
	elle	she
	on	one

Plural

First person	nous	we

Second person	vous	you
Third person	ils (m)	they
	elle (f)	they

Examples:

Dean étudie.	Dean is studying.
Il étudie.	He is studying.

Mes parents habitent en Mexique.	My parents live in Mexico.
Ils habitent en Mexique.	They live in Mexico.

The subject pronoun "je" is used a lot like "I", its English equivalent. Unlike "I", however, "je" is only capitalized when used at the start of a sentence.

Je nettoyer ma chambre tous les jours.	I clean my room every day.
Je veux voir ce film.	I want to see this movie.
Tu sais, j'ai une réservation.	You know, I have a reservation.

When it is placed before a vowel or mute h, "je" must be contracted to "j"

J'ai regardé un film.	I watched a movie.
Oui, j'habite en Espagne.	Yes, I live in Spain.

While English uses the pronoun "you" to refer to the second person in all cases, in French, there are two ways to use the equivalent pronouns for "you".

"Tu" is used to address a second person in a familiar way. It is used when speaking to a relative, friend, colleague, child, or pet.

"Vous", the plural form, is also the formal of "you" and it is used to show respect or formality with someone. Use "vous" when talking to an older person, someone in authority, a person you don't know well, and anybody else to whom you want to show respect.

The third person subject pronouns "il" and "elle" are used exactly like their English counterparts "he" and "she". Both "il" and "elle" can likewise mean "it". "Il" is also used in weather expressions.

Nouns are either masculine or feminine and the subject pronouns used to replace them in a sentence must agree with the gender.

The indefinite pronoun "on" is the equivalent of "one" and it is frequently used to portray the passive voice. In addition, it is used as an informal replacement for "someone", "we", "you", "they" or people in a general sense.

En France on aime bien manger.	In France one like to eat well.
On a trouvé un sac à main.	A handbag was found.

The subject pronoun "nous" is used like "we" in English.

Nous sommes étudiants.	We are students.
Je l'espère, nous pouvons être des amis.	I hope we can be friends.

The plural subject pronouns "ils" and "elles" both mean "they".

"Ils" is used for groups of men, mixed-gender groups, and combined groups of masculine nouns and mixed masculine-feminine nouns.

"Elles", on the other hand, is used only to refer to all-female or groups of feminine nouns.

Direct Objects and Direct Object Pronouns

Direct objects are the 'receiver' of the action of a verb and they answer the question "whom?" or "what?" after an action verb.

Vous devez apprendre ces règles de grammaire.
You must learn these grammar rules.

Je vois Marie.
I see Marie.

Direct object pronouns are words that take the place of direct objects.

Singular

me/m'	me
te/t'	you
le/l'	him, it
la/l'	her, it

Plural

nous	us
vous	you
les	them

"Me", "te", "le" and "la" form elisions when they precede a vowel or mute h. Direct object pronouns are placed before the verb.

Il nous aime.	He loves us.
Elle m'écoute.	She listens to me.
Je le mange.	I eat it.

Indirect Objects and Indirect Object Pronouns

Indirect objects tell for whom, for what, or to whom the action of the verb is done.

Nous parlons à la foule.	We talked to the crowd.
Je parle à <u>Pierre</u>.	I'm talking to Pierre.

Indirect object pronouns are words that take the place of indirect objects and they can only refer to a person or other animate noun.

Singular

me/m'	me
te/t'	you
lui	him, her

Plural

nous	us
vous	you
leur	them

"Me" and "te" form elisions when they precede a vowel or mute h. Indirect object pronouns are generally placed before the verb.

Nous leur parlons.	We talked to them.
Je vous donne le pain.	I'm giving the bread to you.
Ils lui ressemblent.	They resemble him.
Elle m'a écrit.	She wrote to me.

An indirect object pronoun can only be used to replace an animate indirect object, that is, a person or an animal. If the indirect object is inanimate, it is replaced by the adverbial pronoun "y".

Vous y répondez. (à la question)	You respond to it.

In most tenses and moods, and with most verbs, an indirect object pronoun in the first or second person has to precede the verb.

Il me parle.	He is talking to me.

Reflexive Pronouns

A Reflexive pronoun is a special type of pronoun that can only be used with a pronominal verb. A reflexive pronoun is needed when the subject performing the action is the same as the object receiving the action of the verb. The number and gender of the reflexive pronoun should match those of the subject of the verb.

"Me", "te" and "se" are contracted when placed before a vowel of a mute h. "Toi" is used in place of "te" when used in the imperative.

Reflexive pronouns must agree with their subjects in all tenses and moods.

Singular

me, m'	me, myself
te, t', toi	you, yourself
se, s'	him(self), her(self), it(self), them(selves)

Plural

nous	us, ourselves
vous	you, yourself, yourselves

Examples:

Nous nous parlons.	We're talking to each other.
Ils se douchent chaque matin.	They shower every morning.
Je me réveille à 7 heures.	I wake up at 7 o'clock.
Nous nous sommes couchés.	We went to bed.

Here are the most common pronominal (reflexive) verbs that require reflexive pronouns:

se souvenir de	to remember
se doucher	to take a shower
s'habiller	to dress oneself
se brosser (les dents)	to brush (one's teeth)
se déshabiller	to undress oneself
se réveiller	to wake up
s'asseoir	to sit down
se coucher	to go to bed
se casser (un os)	to break (a bone)
se marier	to get married

Disjunctive pronouns (Pronoms disjoints)

A disjunctive pronoun or stressed pronoun emphasizes a noun or pronoun that pertains to a person.

French	English
moi	me
toi	you
lui	him
elle	her
soi	oneself
nous	us
vous	you
eux (masculine)	them
elles (feminine)	them

Disjunctive pronouns are used in the following ways:

To emphasize nouns and pronouns

Elle est venue à moi.	She came to me
Je pense à toi.	I'm thinking of you

After c'est and ce sont

Il est plus jeune que moi.	He's younger than me
Ce sont elles qui aiment Paris.	They love Paris.

To specify individual parts when there is more than one subject or object

Eux et moi, on se voit souvent.	They and I see each other a lot.
Mariel et moi jouons au tennis.	Mariel and I are playing tennis.

To ask and answer questions

Qui l'a pris? Moi!	Who's taken it? Me!
Qui va à la plage?	Who is going to the beach?
Lui.	He is.

After Prepositions

C'est à moi.	It's mine, It belongs to me.
Louis habite chez elle.	Louis lives at her house.

After "que" in comparisons

Il est plus jeune que moi.	He's younger than me.
Il travaille plus que moi.	He works more than I (do).

Combined with emphatic words like "aussi", "seul", "non plus", and "surtout"

Eux aussi l'ont essayé.	They tried it too.
Lui seul a travaillé hier.	He alone worked yesterday.

Used with -même(s) for emphasis

Tu l'as vraiment fait toi-même?	You really did it (all by) yourself?
Nous le ferons nous-mêmes.	We'll do it ourselves.

To indicate possession when used after the preposition "à"

C'est à moi.	It's mine, It belongs to me.
Quel livre est à toi?	Which book is yours?

To provide a subject or a pronoun

Lui, je ne l'aime pas du tout.	I don't like him at all.
Moi, je ne suis pas d'accord.	I don't agree.

"Soi" is the third person indefinite disjunctive pronoun which is used only for unspecified persons with an impersonal verb or indefinite pronoun. "Soi" is the equivalent of "one" or "oneself."

Chacun pour soi.	Every man for himself.
Tout le monde l'a fait soi-même	Everyone did it himself

Impersonal Pronouns

Unlike a personal pronoun, an impersonal pronoun doesn't change according to grammatical persons. Some of them, however, change to conform to the number and gender of the noun that they replace.

Here are the impersonal pronouns:
    Adverbials
    Demonstratives
    Indefinite demonstratives
    Indefinites
    Interrogatives
    Negatives
    Possessives
    Relatives
    Indefinite relatives
    Subjects

Adverbials   (y, en)

The adverbial pronoun "y" is a tiny yet extremely significant part of a sentence. "Y" refers to an implied, obvious, or previously mentioned place and it is most commonly used as an equivalent to the English "there". "Y" usually replaces a preposition of place as well as the place itself.

In general, "y" is placed immediately before the verb. It comes before the infinitive if there is one. In the absence of an infinitive, "y" is placed before the conjugated verb. The word "y" acts as a vowel and so requires a liaison.

Je vais au cinéma.	I am going to the movies.

Nous y allons à 15h00.	We are going there at 3:00p.m.

Nous allons au magasin.	We're going to the store.
Tu veux y aller?	Do you want to go (there)?

Il va au Canada.	He is going to Canada.
Il y va demain.	He is going there tomorrow.

"Y" can also be used to replace "à" + a non-person pronoun.

Tu dois obéir à la loi.	You have to obey the law.
Tu dois y obéir.	You have to obey it.

Je pense à ta décision.	I'm thinking about your decision.
J'y pense tout le temps.	I'm thinking about it all the time.

"Y" can be used to replace "à" + person in cases where indirect object pronouns cannot be placed before the verb.

Fais attention à elle, Fais-y attention.	Pay attention to her.

The adverbial pronoun "en" is used in place of the "de"+indefinite article+noun or partitive article+noun or. It is the equivalent of the English words "any", "some", or "one".

Maman fait des biscuits.	Mom is making some cookies.
Tu en veux?	Do you want some/any?
Il a envie d'une pomme.	He wants an apple.
Il en a envie.	He wants one.

In sentences with a noun that follows an adverb of quantity or a number, "en" is used to replace the noun. In such cases, the adverb of quantity or number is moved to the end of the sentence.

Tu as mangé un sandwich et j'en ai mangé trois.	You ate a sandwich and I ate three (of them).

Demonstrative pronouns refer to a noun previously mentioned in a sentence. They must agree in number and gender with the nouns they replace. These pronouns are the equivalent of "this one", "these", "those", "the one(s)", and "that one" in the English language.

celui	masculine singular
celle	feminine singular
ceux	masculine plural
celles	feminine plural

Demonstrative pronouns cannot stand alone and can only be used in certain constructions.

1. With the suffixes –ci (here) and –là (there), a demonstrative pronoun is used to distinguish between this one and that one.

Quel garçon aimes-tu? Celui-ci ou celui-là?	Which boy do you like, this one or that one?
Je ne sais pas si je veux ceux-ci ou ceux-là.	I don't know if I want these or those.

2. In a prepositional phrase, it is commonly used with "de" to indicate origin or possession:

Mes amis visitent. Celui de la Grèce et celui d'Espagne.	My friends are visiting, the one from Greece and the one from Spain.

Oui, mais je préfère celui de Adolphe à celui de Adrien.	Yes, but I prefer that of Adolphe to that of Adrien.

3. Demonstrative pronouns help introduce a relative pronoun with a dependent clause. It is most often used in combination with "qui" to say "the one who…" or "those who…"

Celui qui a menti sera puni.	The one who lied will be punished.
Ceux qui travaillent vont devenir riche.	Those who work will get rich.

Indefinite pronouns (Pronoms indéfinis)

Indefinite pronouns replace nouns but do not specify which noun they replace whether it be: the subject of a sentence, the object of a preposition, or the object of a verb.

un(e) autre	another one
d'autres	others
soi	oneself
tel	one, someone
tout	everything
tout le monde	everyone
certain(e)s	certain ones
chacun(e)	each one
on	one (subject)
un, l'un	one, the one
plusieurs	several
quelque chose	something

quelqu'un	someone
quelques-uns	some, a few
quiconque	anyone

Personne ne peut traverser le pont.	No one can cross the bridge.
J'ai un cadeau pour quelqu'un.	I have a gift for someone.

"On", the indefinite subject pronoun, literally means "one" and it is often equivalent to the passive voice in the English language. Likewise, it is used as an informal replacement for "someone", "we", "you", "they" or people in general.

Ici on parle français.	French is spoken here.
On a trouvé mon portefeuille.	Someone found my wallet.

Interrogative Pronouns

There are three interrogative pronouns in French and they are used to ask questions using either "est-ce que", or subject-verb inversion in cases where "que" is an object: "qui", "que", and "lequel".

"Qui" translates as "who" or "whom" and it is used when asking about people.

Avec qui aimeriez-vous parler?	With whom would you like to speak?
Qui est-ce que tu vois?	Whom do you see?

When the subject of the question is "who", either "qui" or "qui est-ce qui" can be used. In such cases, the verb is always in the third person singular and the word order is invariable.

Qui parle? (Qui est-ce qui parle?)	Who is speaking?
Qui gagne?	Who is winning?

"Qui" can likewise be used after a preposition.

| De qui dépends-tu? | Upon whom do you depend? |

"Que" translates as "what" and it is used to refer to ideas or objects. When "what" is the object of the question, "que" is commonly followed by "est-ce que" or inversion (when the normal word sequence is inverted to verb+subject).

| Qu'est-ce qu'il veut? | What is it that he wants? |
| Qu'est-ce que tu penses de mon idée? | What do you think of my idea? |

When the subject of the question is "what", "qu'est-ce qui" + a third person singular verb must be used with no inversion.

When it follows a preposition, "que" changes to "quoi"

| En quoi pense-elle? | What is she thinking about? |
| À quoi est-ce qu'il travaille? | What's he working on? |

Negative Pronouns (Pronoms negatives)

Negative pronouns refute, negate, or cast doubt on the existence of the noun they stand for. They can function as a subject, direct object, or indirect object in a sentence.

French negative pronouns are also called indefinite negative pronouns and are made of two parts that are placed before and after the verb. They are very similar to negative adjectives and in fact, all negative adjectives can be found in the list of negative pronouns:

| ne... aucun(e) (de) | none (of), not any (of) |

ne... nul(le)	no one
ne... pas un(e) (de)	not one (of)
ne... pas un(e) seul(e) (de)	not a single one (of)
ne... personne	no one
ne... quiconque	no one
ne... rien	nothing, not... anything

Il ne pense à rien.	He's not thinking about anything.
Il ne veut parler à personne.	He does not want to talk to anybody.

In dual-verb or compound verbs constructions, most negative pronouns are placed around the conjugated first verb.

Je n'ai rien vu.	I didn't see anything.

Possessive Pronouns (Pronoms Possessifs)

Possessive pronouns replace nouns modified by possessive adjectives. French possessive pronouns must agree with the number and gender of the noun being replaced. In addition, the appropriate definite article should be used.

Singular	Singular	Plural	Plural	English
Masculine	Feminine	Masculine	Feminine	English

le mien	la mienne	les miens	les miennes	mine
le tien	la tienne	les tiens	les tiennes	yours ("tu" form)
le sien	la sienne	les siens	les siennes	his/hers/its
le nôtre	la nôtre	les nôtres	les nôtres	ours
le vôtre	la vôtre	les vôtres	les vôtres	yours ("vous" form)
le leur	la leur	les leurs	les leur	theirs

C'est le chat de Adrienne; c'est le sien.	It is Adrienne's cat; it is hers.

Mon père et le vôtre sont partis ensemble.	My father and yours left together.

The prepositions "à" and "de" contract with the definite article when it is placed before a possessive pronoun.

Cet élève est un des miens	This pupil is one of mine

Relative Pronouns (Pronoms relatifs)

Relative pronouns link two ideas together into one sentence by linking a dependent clause to a main clause.

Pronoun	Function(s)	Nearest Translation
Qui	Subject	who, what
	Indirect object (person)	which, that, whom
Que	Direct object	whom, what, which, that
Lequel	Indirect object (thing)	what, which, that
Dont	Object of "de"	of which, from which
	(denote possession)	that, whose
Où	Indicate place or time	when, where, that, which, that

"Qui" replaces the subject (person or object) of a dependent clause and must agree in number with its antecedent. It is likewise used to replace an indirect object.

J'ai lu une livre qui m'a beaucoup amuse.	I read a book that entertained me a great deal.

"Que" functions as the direct object of a clause and it is followed by a subject instead of a verb. With "que", the -e is removed as an elision is made with a vowel.

J'ai acheté le livre que ma tante a écrit.	I bought the book (that) my aunt wrote.

L'actrice américaine qu'il adore s'appelle Meryl Streep.	The American actress he loves is named Meryl Streep.

In general, "lequel" is used to replace the inanimate object of a preposition except when the preposition is "de" in which case the relative pronoun "don't" is used. "Lequel" changes in form to agree with the number and gender of the noun to which it refers. Like the definite article, it can contract with "à" and "de".

L'endroit à laquelle je songe...	The place about which I'm dreaming...

Chapter 13: Adjectives (Adjectifs)

An adjective is a word that describes of modifies a noun or a pronoun. French adjectives differ from English adjectives because they must change in form to agree with the number and gender of the noun that they modify. In addition, most French adjectives follow the noun they modify.

Most adjectives form their feminine by adding an "e" to its masculine form. When the "e" follows a vowel, there is no change in pronunciation but when it is added after a consonant, a change in pronunciation occurs resulting in the pronunciation of the consonant.

Masculine	Feminine	Meaning
grand [grahN]	grande [grahNd]	big
occupé [oh-kew-pay]	occupée [oh-kew-pay]	busy
bleu [bluh]	bleue [bluh]	blue
blond [blohN]	blonde [blohNd]	blond
charmant [shahr-mahN]	charmante [shahr-mahNt]	charming
dévoué [day-voo-ay]	dévouée [day-voo-ay]	devoted
élégant [ay-lay-gahN]	élégante [ay-lay-gahNt]	elegant
français [frahN-she]	française [frahN-sehz]	French
content [kohN-than]	contente [kohN-tahNt]	glad
lourd [loor]	lourde [lord]	heavy
prochain [proh-shahN]	prochaine [proh-shehn]	next
âgé [ah-zhay]	âgée [ah-zhay]	old, aged
ouvert [oo-vehr]	ouverte [oo-vehrt]	open
poli [poh-lee]	polie [poh-lee]	polite
joli [zhoh-lee]	jolie [zhoh-lee]	pretty
parfait [pahr-feh]	parfaite [pahr-feht]	perfect
situé [see-tew-ay]	située [see-tew-ay]	situated

court [koor]	courte [koort]	short
fort [fohr]	forte [fohrt]	strong
petit [puh-tee]	petite [puh-teet]	small
fatigué [fah-tee-gay]	fatiguée [fah-tee-gay]	tired
haut [o]	haute [ot]	tall, big

Adjectives Ending -f and -ve

Masculine adjectives ending –f form the feminine by changing -f to –ve.

Masculine	Feminine	English
actif [ahk-teef]	active [ahk-teev]	active
attentif [ah-tahN-teef]	attentive [ah-tahN-teev]	attentive
impulsif [aN-pewl-seef]	impulsive [aN-pewl-seev]	impulsive
intuitif [aN-tew-ee-teef]	intuitive [aN-tew-ee-teev]	intuitive
naïf [nah-eef]	naïve [nah-eev]	naive
neuf [nuhf]	neuve [nuhv]	new

Adjectives Ending -eux and -euse

Masculine adjectives ending -x form the feminine by changing -x to -se. This gives the feminine ending a "z" sound.

Masculine	Feminine	English
affectueux [ah-fehk-tew-uh]	affectueuse [ah-fehk-tew-uhz]	affectionate
ambitieux [ahN-bee-syuh]	ambitieuse [ahN-bee-syuhz]	ambitious
courageux [koo-rah-zhuh]	courageuse [koo-rah-zhuhz]	courageous
curieux [kew-ryuh]	curieuse [kew-ryuhz]	curious
dangereux [dahNzh-ruh]	dangereuse [dahNzh-ruhz]	dangerous
délicieux [day-lee-syuh]	délicieuse [day-lee-syuhz]	delicious
furieux [few-ryuh]	furieuse [few-ryuhz]	furious

généreux [zhay-nay-ruh	généreuse [zhay-nay-ruhz]	generous
sérieux [say-ryuh]	sérieuse [say-ryuhz]	serious

Adjectives Ending -er and -ère

Masculine adjectives ending -er form the feminine by changing -er to -ère.

Masculine	Feminine	English
cher [shehr]	chère [shehr]	expensive
dernier [dehr-nyay]	dernière [dehr-nyehr]	last
entier [ahN-tyay]	entière [ahN-tyehr]	entire
étranger [ay-trahN-zhay]	étrangère [ay-trahN-zhehr]	foreign
fier [fyehr]	fière [fyehr]	proud
léger [lay-zhay]	légère [lay-zhehr]	light
premier [pruh-myay]	première [puh-myehr]	first

Adjectives that Double Their Consonants

For some masculine adjectives, the feminine is formed by doubling the last consonant and adding -e.

Masculine	Feminine	English
ancien [ahN-syaN]	ancienne [ahN-syehn]	old
bas [bah]	basse [bahs]	low
bon [bohN]	bonne [bohn]	good
européen [ew-roh-pay-aN]	européenne [ew-roh-pay-ehn]	European
gentil [zhahN-tee-y]	gentille [zhahN-tee-y]	nice, kind
gros [gro]	grosse [gros]	fat, big
mignon [mee-nyohN]	mignonne [mee-noyhn]	cute

Irregular Adjectives

Some adjectives take on irregular feminine form and must simply be memorized. Take note that when the adjectives "beau", "nouveau", and "vieux" are placed before masculine nouns that start with a vowel, special forms such as "bel", "nouve", and "vieil" are used respectively.

Masculine	Feminine	English
beau [bo]	belle [behl]	beautiful
blanc [blahN]	blanche [blahNsh]	white
complet [kohN-pleh]	complète [kohN-pleht]	complete
doux [doo]	douce [doos]	sweet
faux [fo]	fausse [fos]	false
favori [fah-voh-ree]	favorite [fah-voh-reet]	favorite
frais [freh]	fraîche [frehsh]	fresh
long [lohN]	longue [lohNg]	long
nouveau [noo-vo]	nouvelle [noo-vehl]	new
vieux [vyuh]	vieille [vyay]	old

Chapter 14: Verbs

Most French verbs fall into one of three categories or families: the -er family, the -ir family, and the -re family. Verbs that belong to a family are classified as regular verbs while verbs that do not belong to any family are called irregular verbs. Each family is governed by separate set of rules.

French verbs are conjugated in four simple tenses, four moods, and in six persons. Conjugation is done by dropping the verb-ending to form the stem and adding a new ending.

The –ER Verbs

Conjugation of -ER Verbs in the Present Tense:

Parler (to talk)

je parle	I talk
tu parles	you talk
il parle	he talks
nous parlons	we talk
vous parlez	you talk
ils parlent	they talk

Donner (to give)

je donne	I give
tu donnes	you give
il donne	he gives
nous donnons	we give
vous donnez	you give
ils donnent	they give

Common -ER Verbs

aider	[eh-day]	to help
annoncer	[ah-nohN-say]	to announce
bavarder	[bah-vahr-day]	to chat
changer	[shahN-zhay]	to change
chercher	[shehr-shay]	to look for
commencer	[koh-mahN-say]	to begin
danser	[dahN-say]	to dance
demander	[duh-mahN-day]	to ask
dépenser	[day-pahN-say]	to spend (money)
donner	[doh-nay]	to give
écouter	[ay-koo-tay]	to listen (to)
étudier	[ay-tew-dyay]	to study
expliquer	[eks-plee-kay]	to explain
exprimer	[eks-pree-may]	to express
fermer	[fehr-may]	to close
fonctionner	[fohNk-syohN-nay]	to function
garder	[gahr-day]	to keep, watch
habiter	[ah-bee-tay]	to live (in)
indiquer	[aN-dee-kay]	to indicate
jouer	[zhoo-ay]	to play
laver	[lah-vay]	to wash
manger	[mahN-zhay]	to eat
marcher	[mahr-shay]	to walk
nager	[nah-zhay]	to swim
oublier	[oo-blee-yay]	to forget
parler	[pahr-lay]	to speak
penser	[pahN-say]	to think

préparer	[pray-pah-ray]	to prepare
présenter	[pray-zahN-tay]	to present, introduce
quitter	[kee-tay]	to leave, remove
regarder	[ruh-gahr-day]	to look at, watch
regretter	[ruh-gruh-tay]	to regret
rencontrer	[rahN-kohN-tray]	to meet
retourner	[ruh-toor-nay]	to return
sembler	[sahN-blay]	to seem
signer	[see-nyay]	to sign
téléphoner	[tay-lay-foh-nay]	to telephone
travailler	[trah-vah-yay]	to work
voyager	[vwah-yah-zhay]	to travel

The –IR Verbs

Conjugation of -IR Verbs in the Present Tense

Choisir (to choose)

je choisis	I choose
tu choisis	you choose
il choisit	he chooses
nous choisissons	we choose
vous choisissez	you choose
ils choisissent	they choose

Finir (to finish)

je finis	I finish
tu finis	you finish
il finit	he finishes
nous finissons	we finish
vous finissez	you finish
ils finissent	they finish

Common -IR Verbs

agir	[ah-zheer]	to act
avertir	[ah-vehr-teer]	to warn
blanchir	[blahN-sheer]	to bleach, to whiten
choisir	[shwah-zeer]	to choose
finir	[fee-neer]	to finish
guérir	[gay-reer]	to cure
jouir	[zhoo-eer]	to enjoy

maigrir	[meh-greer]	to become thin
obéir	[oh-bay-eer]	to obey
punir	[pew-neer]	to punish
réfléchir	[ray-flay-sheer]	to reflect, to think
réussir	[ray-ew-seer]	to succeed

The —RE Verbs

Conjugation of -RE Verbs in the Present Tense

Descendre (to descend)

je descends	I descend.
tu descends	you descend
il descend	he descends
nous descendons	we descend
vous descendez	you descend
ils descendent	they descend

Perdre (to lose)

je perds	I lose
tu perds	you lose
il perd	he loses
nous perdons	we lose
vous perdez	you lose
ils perdent	they lose

Common -Re Verbs

attendre	[ah-tahNdr]	to wait (for)
descendre	[deh-sahNdr]	to go (come) down
entendre	[ahN-tahNdr]	to hear
perdre	[pehrdr]	to lose
répondre	[ray-pohNdr]	to answer
vendre	[vahNdr]	to see

Irregular Verbs

The most common irregular verbs are "être", "avoir", "aller", and "faire".

Être (to be)

je suis	[zhuh swee]	I am
tu es	[tew eh]	you are
il, elle, on est	[eel (ehl) (ohN) eh]	he, she, one is
nous sommes	[noo sohm]	we are
vous êtes	[voo zeht]	you are
ils, elles sont	[eel (ehl) sohN]	they are

Adjectives which follow the verb être should agree with the subject.

Examples:

Tu es belle.	You are pretty.
Il est beau.	He is handsome.
Il est fort.	He is strong.
Elles sont belles.	They are pretty.
Nous sommes jeunes.	We are young.
Il est gentil.	He is nice.
Elle est gentille.	She is nice.
Il est méchant.	He is mean.
Elle est méchante.	She is mean.
Je suis content.	I am happy.
Elle est contente.	She is happy.
Il est calme.	He is relaxed.
Il est en colère.	He is angry.

Avoir (to have)

j'ai	[zhay]	I have
tu as	[tew ah]	you have
il, elle, on a	[eel, (ehl), (ohN) ah]	he, she, one has
nous avons	[noo zah-vohN]	we have
vous avez	[voo zah-vay]	you have
ils, elles ont	[eel, (ehlz) ohN]	they have

Aller (to go)

je vais	[zhuh veh]	I go
tu vas	[tew vah]	you go
il, elle, on va	[eel, (ehl) (ohN) vah]	he, she, one goes
nous allons	[noo zah-lohN]	we go
vous allez	[voo zah-lay]	you go
ils, elles vont	[eel (ehl) vohN]	they go

Faire (to make, to do)

je fais	[zhuh feh]	I make, do
tu fais	[tew feh]	you make, do
il, elle, on fait	[eel (ehl, ohN) feh]	he (she, one) makes, does
nous faisons	[noo fuh-zohN]	we make, do
vous faites	[voo feht]	you make, do
ils, elles font	[eel (ehl) fohN]	they make, do

Idioms using "Faire":

faire attention à	[fehr ah-tahN-syohN ah]	to pay attention to
faire exprès	[fehr ehks-preh]	to do on purpose
faire la queue	[fehr lah kuh]	to stand in line
faire une partie de	[fehr ewn pahr-tee duh]	to play a game of
faire une promenade	[fehr ewn prohm-nahd]	to take a walk

faire un voyage	[fehr uhN vwah-yahzh]	to take a trip
faire venir	[fehr vuh-neer]	to send for

"Pouvoir", "Vouloir", "Savoir" and "Devoir" – The Modal Accessories

Pouvoir (to be able to, can)

je peux	[zhuh puh]	I am able to, I can
tu peux	[tew puh]	you are able to, you can
il, elle, on peut	[eel, ehl, ohN puh]	he, she, one is able to/ he, she, it can
nous pouvons	[noo poo-vohN]	we are able to, we can
vous pouvez	[voo poo-vay]	you are able to, you can
ils, elles peuvent	[eel, (ehl) puhv]	they are able to, they can

Vouloir (to want)

je veux	[zhuh vuh]	I want
tu veux	[tew vuh]	you want
il, elle, on veut	[eel, ehl, ohN vuh]	he, she, one wants
nous voulons	[noo voo-lohN]	we want
vous voulez	[voo-lay]	you want
ils, elles veulent	[eel (ehl) vuhl]	they want

Savoir (to know)

je sais	[zhuh seh]	I know
tu sais	[tew seh]	you know
il, elle, on sait	[eel, ehl, ohN seh]	he, she, one knows
nous savons	[noo sah-vohN]	we know
vous savez	[voo sah-vez]	you know
ils, elles savent	[eel, ehl sahv]	they know

Devoir (to have to)

je dois	[zhuh dwah]	I have to
tu dois	[tew dwah]	you have to

il, elle, on doit	[eel, ehl, ohN dwah]	he, she, one has to
nous devons	[noo duh-vohN]	we have to
vous devez	[voo duh-vay]	you have to
ils, elles doivent	[eel, ehl dwahv]	they have to

Other Irregular Verbs

Voir (to see)

je vois	[zhuh vwah]	I see
tu vois	[tew vwah]	you see
il, elle, on voit	[eel, ehl, ohN vwah]	he, she, one sees
nous voyons	[noo vwah-yohN]	we see
vous voyez	[voo vwah-yay]	you see
ils, elles voient	[eel, ehl vwah]	they see

Dire (to say, to tell)

je dis	[zhuh dee]	I say, I tell
tu dis	[tew dee]	you say, you tell
il, elle, on dit	[eel, ehl, ohN dee]	he, she, one says/ he, she, one tells
nous disons	[noo dee-zohN]	we say, we tell
vous dites	[voo deet]	you say, you tell
ils, elles disent	[eel, ehl deez]	they say, they tell

Lire (to read)

je lis	[zhuh lee]	I read

tu lis	[tew lee]	you read
il, elle, on lit	[eel, ehl, ohN lee]	he, she, one reads
nous lisons	[noo lee-zohN]	we read
vous lisez	[voo lee-zay]	you read
ils, elles lisent	[eel, ehl leez]	they read

Se sentir (to feel)

je me sens	[zhuh muh sahN]	I feel
tu te sens	[tew tuh sahN]	you feel
il, elle, on se sent	[eel, ehl, ohN suh sahN]	he, she, one feels
nous nous sentons	[noo noo sahN-tohN]	we feel
vous vous sentez	[voo voo sahN-tay]	you feel
ils, elles se sentent	[eel, ehl suh sahNt]	they feel

Venir (to come)

je viens	[zhuh vyaN]	I come
tu viens	[tew vyaN]	you come
il, elle, on vient	[eel (ehl, ohN) vyaN]	he, she, one comes
nous venons	[noo vuh-nohN]	we come
vous venez	[voo vuh-nay]	you come
ils, elles viennent	[eel, ehl vyehn]	they come

Connaître (to know)

je connais	[zhuh koh-neh]	I know
tu connais	[tew koh-neh]	you know
il, elle, on connaît	[eel, ehl, ohN koh-neh]	he, she, one knows
nous connaissons	[noo koh-neh-sohN]	we know

vous connaissez	[voo koh-neh-say]	you know
ils, elles connaissent	[eel, ehl koh-nehs]	they know

Verbs Used to Give Directions

aller	[ah-lay]	to go
continuer	[kohN-tee-new-ay]	to continue
descendre	[day-sahNdr]	to go down
marcher	[mahr-shay]	to walk
monter	[mohN-tay]	to go up
passer	[pah-say]	to pass
prendre	[prahNdr]	to take
tourner	[toor-nay]	to turn
traverser	[trah-vehr-say]	to cross

Chapter 15: Prepositions

Prepositions show the relation of a noun to other words in a sentence. Here is a list of the most commonly used prepositions in French:

French	Pronunciation	English
à	[ah]	to, at
après	[ah-preh]	after
pour	[poor]	for, in order to
avant	[ah-vahN]	before
chez	[shay]	at, at the house of
derrière	[deh-ryehr]	behind
entre	[ahNtr]	between
contre	[kohNtr]	against
dans	[dahN]	in
de	[duh]	from
par	[pahr]	by, through
près (de)	[preh (duh)]	near (to)
devant	[duh-vahN]	in front of
en	[ahN]	in
loin (de)	[lwaN (duh)]	far (from)
sur	[sewr]	on
vers	[vehr]	toward
sans	[sahN]	without
sous	[soo]	under

Prepositions of Location

chez	[shay]	at, at the house of
contre	[kohNtr]	against
dans	[dahN]	in
derrière	[deh-ryehr]	behind
devant	[duh-vahN]	in front of
en	[ahN]	in
entre	[ahNtr]	between
sous	[soo]	under
sur	[sewr]	on
vers	[vehr]	toward

Chapter 16: Transportation

France has world-class public transport in its cities and larger towns. You can rely on their metros, light rails, and buses to take you just about anywhere around the country.

To help you take the train, buses, or taxi, here are some useful phrases.

Bus

Taking the bus is an inexpensive transportation alternative in France. Here are useful phrases to help you get to your destination:

Où est l'arrêt d'autobus?	[oo ay lah-ray doh-toh-bewss]	Where's the bus stop?
Quelle direction dois-je prendre pour aller à ____?	[kell dee-reks-yong dwahzh prahngdr poor ahlay ah]	Which line goes to ____?
Quel bus dois-je prendre pour aller à ____?	[kell bewss dwahzh prahng dr poor ahlay ah]	Which bus do I take to go to ____?
Un ticket, s'il vous plaît.	[ang tee-kay seel voo play]	A ticket, please.

Taxi

Où est-ce que je peux trouver un taxi?	[oo essker zher per troo-vay ang taxee]	Where can I find a taxi?
Est-ce que vous pouvez m'emmener à cette adresse?	[essker voo poovay mahng m-nay ah set ah-dress]	Can you take me to this address?
Je suis pressé(e).	[zher swee pray-say]	I'm in a hurry.
Pouvez-vous m'attendre?	[poovay voo mah-tahngdr]	Could you wait for me?

Je reviens dans deux minutes.	[zher rer-vyang dahng der mee-newt]	I'll be back in two minutes.
La gare, s'il vous plaît.	[lah gahr seel voo play]	To the station, please.
Le centre ville, s'il vous plaît.	[ler sahngtr veel seel voo play]	The city centre, please.
L'aéroport, s'il vous plaît.	[lay-ay-roh-por seel voo play]	To the airport, please.
C'est ici.	[sayt ee cee]	It's here.
Combien est-ce que je vous dois?	[kong-byang essker zher voo dwah]	How much is it?
Tout droit.	[too drwah]	Straight ahead.
À gauche ici.	[ah gosh ee-see]	Left here.
À droite ici.	[ah drwah tee-see]	Right here.

Train

Où est le guichet?	[oo ay ler ghee-shay]	Where's the ticket office?
À quelle heure est-ce qu'il arrive, ce train?	[ah kell err ess kee lah-reev, ser trang]	What time does the train arrive?
Quel est le tarif jusqu'a Paris?	[kell ay ler tah-reef zhew-skah pah-ree]	How much is the fare to Paris?
Je voudrais réserver une place.	[zher voodray ray-zair-vay ewn plahss]	I'd like to reserve a seat.

Signs/Useful Terms at the Train Station

arrivée/départ Grandes Lignes	arrivals/departures main-lines
arrivée/départ Banlieue	arrivals/departures suburbs
un aller simple	a one way ticket
un aller et retour	a round trip ticket
entrée	entrance
sortie	exit
renseignements	information
composter votre billet	punch (validate) your ticket
accès aux quais	access to platforms

Modes of Transportation

en automobile	[ahN no-toh-moh-beel]	by car
en bus	[ahN bews]	by bus
à bicyclette	[ah bee-see-kleht]	by bicycle
à cheval	[ah shuh-vahl]	on horseback
à moto	[ah moh-to]	by scooter
à pied	[ah pyeh]	on foot
en avion	[ahN nah-vyohN]	by plane
en bateau	[ahN bah-to]	by boat
en métro	[ahN may-tro]	by subway
en taxi	[ahN tahk-see]	by taxi
en train	[ahN traN]	by train
en voiture	[ahN vwah-tewr]	by car

Places to Visit

la plage	[lah plahzh]	beach
le parcours	[luh pahr-koor]	course (golf)
le court	[luh koort]	court
le terrain	[luh teh-raN]	field
le gymnase	[luh zheem-nahz]	gymnasium
la montagne	[mohN-tah-nyuh]	mountain
l'océan (m.)	[loh-see-ahN]	ocean
le parc	[luh pahrk]	park
le sentier	[luh sahN-tyay]	path
la piscine	[lah pee-seen]	pool
la patinoire	[lah pah-tee-nwahr]	rink
la mer	[lah mehr]	sea
la piste	[lah peest]	slope
le stade	[luh stahd]	stadium
la piste	[lah peest]	track

Chapter 17: Ordering Food at Restaurants

French cuisine is one of the best in the world and you will surely partake in the fun of dining out whether you're on a quick visit or planning to live in a French-speaking country. In this section, you will learn essential phrases to order food in restaurants and cafes.

You can tell somebody you're hungry by saying, "j'ai faim" (zheh fehm) which translates as "I'm hungry". You can ask somebody if he or she is hungry by saying, "êtes-vous affamé" (eh-teh-voo ah-fah-meh) which means "Are you hungry?"

You can tell someone you're thirsty with "J'ai soif". To ask somebody if he or she is thirsty, say "avez-vous soif?"

The three main meals (repas) of the day are:

le petit déjeuner [luh puh-tee day-zhuh-nay]	breakfast
le déjeuner [luh day-zhuh-nay]	lunch
le diner [luh dee-nay]	dinner

A traditional full course meal may include appetizer, soup, fish, meat, cheese, dessert and drinks. Most French restaurants offer three or four course fixed-price meals with soup or appetizer and do away with the cheese course. Diners can also choose to order "à la carte" dishes as well as daily specials. A service charge is often included in the price of fixed-priced meals.

After being seated and given a few minutes to peruse the menu, you can call the attention of the server by saying "s'il vous plait" or "please". It is considered rude to use "garcon!" to call their attention. The waiter/waitress will most likely ask one of these questions:

Est-ce que vous voulez commander?	Would you like to order?
Qu'est-ce que vous voudrez?	What would you like to order?
Que voulez-vous?	What would you like?
Voulez-vous une entrée?	Would you like a starter?
Qu'est-ce que vous voulez commander?	What would you like to order?
Oui, s'il vous plaît?	Yes, please?

You can answer with any of these phrases:

Je voudrais de l'eau.	[zhuh-voo-dreh- dehl-oh]	I would like some water.
Quel est le plat du jour?	[kehl eh leh plah dew zhoor]	What is today's special?
Qu'est-ce que vous recommandez?	[kehs-kuh voo ruh-koh-mah-day]	What do you recommend?
Je voudrais _____.	[zhuh-voo-dreh]	I would like _____.

Here are terms you will find useful in going over the menu:

à prix fixe	[a pree feex]	fixed-price
le menu	[muh-new]	set menu
la carte	[lah kahrt]	the menu
les entrées	[lay zohn-tray]	appetizers
le dessert	[leh deh-ser]	the desert
le plat du jour	[leh plah dew zhoor]	the dish of the day
le plat principal	[leh plah prahn-see-pal]	the main course
la carte des vins	[lah kahrt deh va]	the wine list
à la carte	[ah lah kahrt]	ordered separately
le plat du jour	[luh plah dew zhoor]	the daily special

service compris	[sehr-vees koh-pree]	service charge included
boisson compris	[bwah-soh (va) koh-pree]	beverage included
l'assiette de fromage	[lah-see-eht duh froh-mahzh]	cheeseplate
la spécialité de la maison	[lah spay-see-ah-lee-tay duh lah meh-zoh]	house special

Beverages (les boissons)

Common choices for drinks are aperitifs, wine and mineral water. Here are some terms you can use in making your beverage order.

Quelque chose à boire?	[kehl-kuh shohz ah bwahr]	Something to drink?
une bouteille	[ewn boo-tay]	a bottle
une carafe	[ewn kah-rahf]	a carafe
un pichet	[uh pee-sheh]	a jug
un demi-litre	[uh duh-mee-leetr(uh)]	a ½ liter
un quart (litre)	[uh kahr [leetr(uh)]	a ¼ liter
un verre	[uh vehr]	a glass
une bouteille du vin	[ewn boo-tay dew vahn]	a bottle of wine
une tasse de café	[ewn tas deh kah-fay]	a cup of coffee
une tasse de thé	[ewn tas deh tay]	a cup of tea
un verre d'eau	[uhn vair duh]	a glass of water
l'eau minérale	[loh mee-nay-rahl]	mineral water
le vin rouge	[luh va roozh]	red wine
le vin blanc	[luh va blah]	white wine
le vin rosé	[luh va roh-zay]	rosé wine
le vin mousseux	[leh vihn moo-soh]	sparkling wine
le champagne	[luhshahm-PAH-nyuh]	champagne
la bière	[lahbyehr]	beer
la bière brune	[lah bee-yehr brewn]	dark beer
la bière blonde	[lah bee-yehr blohnd]	light beer
la bière à la pression	[lah bee-yehr ah lah pres-see-ohn]	tap beer
le café crème	[leh ka-fay krem]	coffee with cream
le café au lait	[leh ka-fay oh lay]	coffee with milk
le café noir	[leh ka-fay nwahr]	black coffee
le café décaféiné	[leh ka-fay day-kah-fay-nay]	decaf coffee
le café glacé	[leh ka-fay gla-say]	iced coffee

les boissons	[lay bwah-sohn]	drinks
le café espresso	[leh ka-fay ek-spray-so]	espresso
le digestif, la liqueur	[leh dee-gest-teef]	liqueur
le lait	[leh lay]	milk
le café oh chocolat	[leh ka-fay oh show-koh-lah]	chocolate milk
le jus d'orange	[leh juj doh-rahnzj]	orange juice
le thé	[leh tay]	tea
le thé au citron	[leh tay oh see-trohn]	tea with lemon
le thé sucré	[leh tay sue-kray]	tea with sugar
la tisane	[lah tee-zan]	herbal tea
le thé glace	[leh tay gla-say]	iced tea
l'eau	[low]	water
l'eau du robinet	[low dew row-bee-nay]	tap water

After getting your beverage order, you will now be asked for your food choices. You can use the following terms to describe how you want your word to be prepared:

chaud	[sho]	warm, hot
petit	[puh-teet]	small, short
grand	[grahNd]	big, tall, large
froid	[frwah]	cold

Usefule Words or Phrases for Ordering Food:

un plat	[uh plah]	a dish
la soupe	[lah soop]	soup
le potage	[luh poh-tahzh]	creamy soup
l'entrée (f.)	[lon-tray]	appetizer
la viande	[lah vee-yahd]	meat
le poisson	[luh pwah-soh]	fish
les légumes (m.)	[lah lay-gewm]	vegetables
le fromage	[luh froh-mazh]	cheese
le dessert	[luh day-sehr]	dessert
de l'eau	[duh loh]	some water
encore du pain	[ah-kohr dew pa]	more bread
encore du vin	[ah-kohr dew va]	more wine
ça suffit	[sah sew-fee]	that's enough

Here are usual appetizers you might see on the menu:

les canapés (m.) [kah-nah-pay]	small snacks or pieces of bread or pastry with delectable toppings
les crudités (f) [krew-dee-tay]	assorted raw or lightly blanched

	vegetables dipped in a vinaigrette
le pâté [pah-tay]	ground meat, vegetables, and herbs minced into a paste
le pâté de foie gras [luh pah-tay duh fwah grah]	pâté made from duck liver
les escargots à la bourguignonne [les ehs-kahr-goh ah lah boor-gee-nyohn]	snails in the shell with butter and garlic

Soup (la soupe)

le consommé [luh koh-soh-may]	clear meat broth
le velouté [luh vuh-loo-taya]	creamy soup
la vichyssoise [lah vee-shee-swahz]	cold leek and potato soup
la soupe à l'oignon [lah soop ah lwah-nyoh]	French onion soup

Fish (les poisons)

le hareng	[luh ah-rah]	herring
la lotte	[lah loht]	monkfish
la moule	[lah mool]	mussel
l'huître	[luh-weetr(uh)]	oyster
le saumon	[luh soh-moh]	salmon
la crevette	[lah kruh-veht]	shrimp
le thon	[luh toh]	tuna

Poultry and Game (la volaille et le gibier)

le suprême de volaille	[luh sew-prehm duh voh-lahy]	chicken breast
le canard	[luh kah-nahr]	duck
l'oie (f.)	[lwah]	goose
le lapin	[luh lah-pa]	rabbit
le pigeon	[luh pee-zhoh]	pigeon
la caille	[lah kahy]	quail
la dinde	[lah dund]	turkey

Meat (la viande)

le boeuf	[luh buhf]	beef
le bifteck	[luh beef-tehk]	beefsteak
le jambon	[luh zhah-boh]	ham
l'agneau (m.)	[lah-nyoh]	lamb
la foie	[lah fwah]	liver
le porc	[luh pohr]	pork
l'entrecôte (f.)	[lon-truh-koht]	rib steak
la saucisse	[lah soh-sees]	sausage
le steak	[luh stehk]	steak
le veau	[luh voh]	veal

Offal (les abats)

le rognon	[luh roh-nyoh]	kidney
la cervelle	[lah sehr-vehl]	brains (lamb or veal)
le ris de veau	[luh ree duh voh]	veal sweetbreads

If you want to tell the server how you want to have your steak done, the following terms may be useful:

bleu	[bluh]	very rare
saignant	[seh-nyah]	rare
à point	[ah pwa]	medium-rare
bien cuit	[byah kwee]	well done

Sauces and Preparations

l'aïoli (m.)	[lah-yoh-lee]	garlic mayonnaise
la sauce béarnaise	[lah sos bay-ahr-nehz]	egg, butter, and wine sauce
le beurre blanc	[leh buhr blah]	butter, shallots, and white wine sauce
la sauce chasseur	[lah sos shah-suhr]	mushrooms, wine, and parsley sauce
le gratin	[luh grah-ta]	crusty baked dish made with cheese
la sauce hollandaise	[lah sos oh-lah-dehz]	butter, egg yolk, and vinegar sauce
la sauce meunière	[la sos muh-nyehr]	butter and lemon sauce
la sauce provençale	[lah sos proh-vah-sahl]	tomatoes, anchovies and garlic sauce

Desserts

la crème bavaroise	[lah krehm bah-vahr-wahz]	Bavarian cream
la charlotte	[lah shahr-loht]	trifle made with lady fingers
la crème caramel	[lah krehm kah-rah-mehl]	egg custard with caramel sauce
la crème brûlée	[lah krehm brew-lay]	custard topped with hard caramel
les crêpes suzettes	[leh krehp sew-zeht]	crêpes with caramelized sugar
la mousse au chocolat	[lah moos oh shoh-koh-lah]	chocolate mousse
la tarte tatin	[lah tahrt tah-ta]	caramelized apple tart
les profiteroles	[leh proh-fee-tuh-rohl]	creamy pastry chocolate sauce
le sorbet	[leh sohr-beh]	sherbet
la glace	[lah glahs]	ice cream

Spices, Condiments, and Herbs

le basilic	[luh bah-zee-leek]	basil
la feuille de laurier	[lah fuhy duh loh-ryay]	bay leaf
le beurre	[luh buhr]	butter
les câpres	[lay kahpr]	capers
la ciboulette	[lah see-boo-leht]	chives
l'aneth	[lah-neht]	dill
l'ail	[lahy]	garlic
le gingembre	[luh zhaN-zhahNbr]	ginger
le miel	[luh myehl]	honey
le raifort	[luh reh-fohr]	horseradish
le ketchup	[luh keht-chuhp]	ketchup
le citron	[luh see-trohN]	lemon
le sirop d'érable	[luh see-roh day-rahbl]	maple syrup
la mayonnaise	[lah mah-yoh-nehz]	mayonnaise
la menthe	[lah mahNt]	mint

la moutarde	[lah moo-tahrd]	mustard
l'huile	[lweel]	oil
l'origan	[loh-ree-gahN]	oregano
le persil	[luh pehr-seel]	parsley
le poivre	[luh pwahvr]	pepper
le sel	[luh sehl]	salt
le sucre	[luh sewkr]	sugar
l'estragon	[lehs-trah-gohN]	tarragon
le vinaigre	[luh vee-nehgr]	vinegar

Paying the Bill

When you're done with your meal and ready to make the payment, you can ask the server for your bill.

Je voudrais payer, s'il vous plaît.	[Je voudrais payer, sell voo pleh]	I would like to pay, please.

L'addition, s'il vous plait.	[lah-dee-syoh seel voo pleh]	The bill, please.

If you want to use your credit card to settle the bill, you can tell the server:

Je voudrais payer avec une carte de crédit.	[Je voudrais payer ewn kahr-tuh duh cray-dee]	I would like to pay with a credit card.

Useful Restaurant Terms:

le serveur, la serveuse	[sehr-vuhr]	waiter, waitress
une cuillère	[ewn kwee-air]	a spoon
une fourchette	[ewn for-shet]	a fork
un couteau	[uhn koo-toe]	a knife
une cuillère	[ewn kwee-air]	a spoon
une table	[ewn tabhl]	a table
une serviette	[ewn sehr-vee-eht]	a napkin
le caissier, la caissière	[kay-syehr]	cashier
les hors-d'oeuvres	[day zor-duhvr]	appetizers

le pourboire	[poor-bwar]	tip
l'addition	[lah-dee-see-yohn]	the bill
la carte des vins	[lah kart day vahn]	the wine list
commander	[cooh-mahn-day]	to order

At the Hotel

J'ai une réservation.	I have a reservation.
Je voudrais faire une réservation.	I'd like to make a reservation.
J'ai retenu deux chambres.	I have reserved for two rooms.
Est-ce que le petit déjeuner est compris?	Is breakfast included?
Excusez-moi, monsieur	Excuse me sir.
Il y a un problème	There's a problem.
Pourriez-vous m'aider?	Can you help me?
Merci beaucoup!	Thanks very much!
Qu'est-ce qui c'est?	What's that?
Ou sont les toilettes?	Where is the bathroom?

Hotel Facilities

le bar [luh bahr]	bar
le centre d'affaires [luh sahNtr dah-fehr]	business center
la caisse [lah kehs]	cashier
le, la concierge [luh, lah kohN-syehrzh]	concierge
le portier [luh pohr-tyay]	doorman
l'ascenseur (m.) [lah-sahN-suhr]	elevator
le club santé [luh klewb sahN-tay]	fitness center
la boutique [lah boo-teek]	gift shop
la gouvernante [lah goo-vehr-nahNt]	maid service
le restaurant [luh rehs-toh-rahN]	restaurant
la piscine [lah pee-seen]	swimming pool
la blanchisserie [lah blahN-shees-ree]	dry cleaning service

Accommodations (House, Apartment, Rooms)

l'appartement [lah-par-tuh-mahN]	apartment
le grenier [luh gruh-nyay]	attic
la climatisation [lah klee-mah-tee-zah-syohN]	air conditioning
le jardin [luh zhahr-daN]	backyard
le balcon [luh bahl-kohN]	balcony
le sous-sol [luh soo-sohl]	basement
la salle de bains [sahl duh baN]	bathroom
la chambre [lah shahNbr]	room, bedroom
la chambre à coucher [lah shahNbr ah koo-shay]	bedroom
le plafond [luh plah-fohN]	ceiling
la penderie [lah pahN-dree]	closet
la garde-robe [lah gahrd-rohb]	closet
la cour [lah koor]	courtyard
la salle de séjour [lah sahl duh say-zhoor]	den
la porte [lah pohrt]	door
la salle à manger [lah sahl ah mahN-zhay]	dining room
l'ascenseur [lah-sahN-suhr]	elevator
la cheminée [lah shuh-mee-nay]	fireplace
le plancher [luh plahN-shay]	floor
l'étage [lay-tahzh]	floor (storey)
le garage [luh gah-rahzh]	garage
au gaz [o gahz]	gas
le rez-de-chaussée [luh rayd-sho-say]	ground floor
le couloir [luh koo-lwahr]	hallway
le chauffage [luh sho-fahzh]	heating
la maison [lah meh-zohN]	house
la cuisine [lah kwee-zeen]	kitchen
la buanderie [lah bwahN-dree]	laundry room

le bail [luh bahy]	lease
le salon [luh sah-lohN]	living room
l'entretien [lahNtr-tyaN]	maintenance
le propriétaire [luh proh-pree-yay-tehr]	owner
l'allée privée [lah-lay pree-vay]	private road
le loyer [luh lwah-yay]	rent
le toit [luh twah]	roof
la pièce, la salle [lah pyehs, lah sahl]	room
la caution [lah ko-syohN]	security deposit
la douche [lah doosh]	shower
l'escalier [lehs-kah-lyay]	stairs
le débarras [luh day-bah-rah]	storage room
le locataire [luh loh-kah-tehr]	tenant
la terrasse [lah teh-rahs]	terrace
la toilette [lah twah-leht]	toilet
la fenêtre [lah fuh-nehtr]	window

Chapter 18: Using Idioms to Express Your Opinions

à vrai dire	[ah vreh deer]	to tell the truth
au contraire	[o kohN-trehr]	on the contrary
bien entendu	[byaN nahN-tahN-dew]	of course
à mon avis	[ah mohN nah-vee]	in my opinion
bon marché	[bohN mahr-shay]	cheap
c'est-à-dire	[seh-tah-deer]	that is to say
cela ne fait rien	[suh-lah nuh feh ryaN]	that doesn't matter
d'accord	[dah-kohr]	agreed, O.K.
bien sûr	[byaN sewr]	of course
cela m'est égal	[suh-lah meh tay-gahl]	I don't care
de mon côté	[duh mohN ko-tay]	as for me, for my part
jamais de la vie	[zhah-meh duh lah vee]	out of the question
n'importe	[nahN-pohrt]	it doesn't matter
ressembler à	[ruh-sahN-blay ah]	to resemble
sans doute	[sahN doot]	without a doubt
tant mieux	[tahN myuh]	so much the better
tant pis	[tahN pee]	bad
tout à fait	[too tah feh]	entirely
tout de même	[too dmehm]	all the same

Useful Phrases to Express Lack of Understanding or Confusion

Excusez-moi.	[ehk-skew-zay (ehk-skewz) mwah]	Excuse me.
Pardon.	[pahr-dohN]	Pardon me.
Je ne comprends pas.	[pas zhuh nuh kohN-prahN pah]	I don't understand.
Répétez, s'il vous plait.	[ray-pay-tay seel voo pleh]	Can you repeat, please.
Parlez plus lentement.	[pahr-lay plew lahNtmahN]	Speak slowly.

Chapter 19: Shopping

Do you prefer to browse in a large, elegant mall or in small boutiques? It's time to pick up some souvenirs of your trip for your family or friends back home and of course, for yourself. This section will help you find the right clothes, accessories, and merchandise by using basic French shopping phrases.

Useful Phrases:

Ça coûte combien?	How much does that cost?
A quelle heure ouvre le magasin?	At what time does the store open?
A quelle heure ferme le magasin?	At what time does the store close?
Je voudrais acheter ces chaussures.	I would like to purchase these shoes.
Vous désirez?	What would you like?
Puis-je vous aider?	Can I help you?
Je cherche une jupe rouge.	I'm looking for a red skirt.
Je vais prendre ceci.	I would like to buy this.
Est-ce que ce pantalon est en solde?	Are these pants on sale?
Le voici!	Here it is!
Combien coûte cette chemise?	How much is this shirt?
Ce sera tout?	Is that all?
Je voudrais payer en liquide.	I'd like to pay in cash.
Je voudrais payer par carte de credit.	I'd like to pay by credit card.
Puis-je commander cela sur l'Internet?	Can I order this online?

Chapter 20: Asking for Directions

Exploring a foreign-speaking country can be an exciting adventure once you know how to ask for directions to help you find your way around the city. Here are some key phrases you can use.

Useful Phrases:

Où?	Where?
Excusez-moi, où est...?	Excuse me, where is...?
Où sont les taxis?	Where are the taxis?
Où est le métro?	Where is the subway?
Où est le bus?	Where is the bus?
Où est la sortie?	Where is the exit?
C'est loin?	Is it far?
C'est près d'ici?	Is it nearby?
Allez tout droit.	Go straight ahead.
Allez par là.	Go that way.
Retournez.	Go back.
Tournez à droite.	Turn right.
Tournez à gauche.	Turn left.
Quel est le prix de la course?	What is the fare?
Arrêtez-vous ici, s'il vous plait.	Stop here, please.
Est-ce que ce bus passe par la rue Mar?	Does this bus go to Mar St.?
nord	north
sud	south
ouest	west
est	east

Location

à côté (de)	[ah ko-tay (duh)]	next to, beside
à la maison	[ah lah meh-zohN]	at home
à part	[ah pahr]	aside
à travers	[ah trah-vehr]	across, through
à droite (de)	[ah drawht (duh)]	to the right (of)
à gauche (de)	[ah gosh (duh)]	to the left (of)
du côté de	[dew ko-tay duh]	in the direction of
au-dessous de	[o duh-soo duh]	beneath, below
au-dessus de	[oduh-sew duh]	above, over
tout près	[too preh]	nearby
en plein air	[ahN pleh nehr]	in the open air
en bas (de)	[ahN bah duh]	at the bottom of
de l'autre côté (de)	[duh lohtr ko-tay (duh)]	on the other side (of)
le long de	[luh lohN duh]	along
à l'étranger	[ah lay-trahN-zhay]	abroad
à la campagne	[ah lah kahN-pahN-nyuh]	in the country
au loin	[o lwaN]	in the distance
au milieu (de)	[o mee-lyuh (duh)]	in the middle (of)
en direction de	[dew ko-tay duh]	in the direction of
en face (de)	[ahN fahs (duh)]	opposite, facing
en haut (de)	[ahN o (duh)]	at the top of
en ville	[ahN veel]	downtown
par ici (là)	[pahr ee-see (lah)]	this way (that way)
tout droit	[too drwah]	straight ahead

Chapter 21: Vocabulary

la librairie	bookstore
la boulangerie	bakery
le marché	market
le supermarché	supermarket
les vêtements (m.) pour femmes	women's clothes
les vêtements (m.) pour hommes	men's clothes
le chemisier, la jupe, la robe	blouse, skirt, dress
le pantalon, la chemise, la cravate	pants, shirt, tie
les chaussures (f.) et les chaussettes (f.)	shoes and socks
les jeans (m.)	jeans
l'argent	money
la caisse	cash register
la carte de crédit	credit card
cher (chère)	expensive
grand(e)(s)	big, tall, large
large(s)	large
marchand(e)(s)	vendor
petit(e)(s)	small, short
le porte-monnaie	wallet
le sac	bag

Clothing (Les Vêtements)

le maillot	[luh mah-yo]	bathing suit
le bikini	[luh bee-kee-nee]	bikini
la ficelle	[lah fee-sehl]	string
la ceinture	[lah saN-tewr]	belt
le slip	[luh sleep]	briefs, panties
les bottes (f.)	[lay boht]	boots
les gants (m.)	[lay gahN]	gloves
le mouchoir	[luh moo-shwahr]	handkerchief
le chapeau	[luh shah-po]	hat
la veste	[lah vehst]	jacket
jacket le blouson	[luh bloo-zohN]	outer
le jean	[luh zheen]	jeans
le survêt	[luh sewr-veh]	track suit, sweat suit
le manteau	[luh mahN-to]	overcoat
le pantalon	[luh pahN-tah-lohN]	pants
le pull	[luh pewl]	pullover
le pyjama	[luh pee-zhah-mah]	pajamas
l'imperméable (m.)	[laN-pehr-may-ahbl]	raincoat
la robe de chambre	[lah rohb duh shahNbr]	robe
les sandales (f)	[lay sahN-dahl]	sandals
l'écharpe (f.)	[lay-shahrp]	scarf
le foulard	[luh foo-lahr]	scarf
la chemise	[lah shuh-meez]	shirt
les chaussures (f.),	[lay sho-sewr]	shoes
les souliers (m.)	[lay sool-lyay]	shoes
le short	[luh shohrt]	shorts
les tennis	[lay tuh-nees]	sneakers
les chaussettes (f.)	[lay sho-seht]	socks
le tee-shirt	[luh tee-shehrt]	T-shirt

le parapluie	[luh pah-rah-plwee]	umbrella
les sous-vêtements (m.)	[lay soo-veht-mahN]	underwear
le gilet	[luh zhee-leh]	vest

Fabric

en cachemire	[ahN kahsh-meer]	cashmere
en velours	[ahN vuh-loor]	corduroy, velvet
en coton	[ahN koh-tohN]	cotton
en jean	[ahN zheen]	denim
en flanelle	[ahN flah-nehl]	flannel
en gabardine	[ahN gah-bahr-deen]	gabardine
en tricot	[ahN tree-ko]	knit
en cuir	[ahN kweer]	leather
en lin	[ahN laN]	linen

Shopping for Food

In France, people prefer to go shopping almost every day to buy the freshest meats and produce. Food shopping can be exciting if you know how to say what you need to buy.

Useful Phrases:

Nous avons besoin des oeufs, du lait, et du pain.	We need eggs, milk, and bread.
Je dois faire les courses.	I have to go grocery shopping.
Nous avons besoins de _____.	We need _____.

Fruits (les fruits)

la pomme	[lah puhm]	Apple
l'abricot (m.)	[lah-bree-koh]	apricot
la banana	[lah bah-nan]	banana
la myrtille	[lah meer-tee-yah]	blueberry
le melon	[luh meh-lohn]	cantaloupe
l'agrume (m.)	[la-groom]	citrus fruit
le noix de coco	[luh nwah deh koh-koh]	coconut
le lait de noix de coco	[luh lay deh nwah deh koh-koh]	coconut milk
la date	[lah daht]	date
le raisin	[luh ray-zehn]	grape
la figue	[lah feeg]	fig
le pamplemousse	[luh pahm-pluh-moose]	grapefruit
le raisin	[luh ray-zehn]	grape
le citron	[luh see-trohn]	lemon
le citron pressé	[luh see-trohn preh-say]	lemon juice
le citron vert	[luh see-trohn vaire]	lime
le melon	[luh meh-lohn]	melon
l'orange (f.)	[lor-an-jhe]	orange
l'orange pressé (f.)	[lor-an-jhe preh-say]	orange juice
la pêche	[lah paysh]	peach
la poire	[lah pwar]	pear
l'ananas (m.)	[lah-na-nah]	pineapple
la prune	[lah prwehn]	plum
la grenade	[lah greh-nad]	pomegranate
le pruneau	[luh prweh-noh]	prune
le raisin sec	[luh ray-zahn sehk]	raisin
la framboise	[lah frahm-bwahz]	raspberry
la fraise	[lah frehz]	strawberry

| la compote | [lah com-poht] | stewed fruit |
| la pastèque | [lah pas-tek] | watermelon |

Vegetables (les légumes)

l'artichaut (m.)	[larh-tee-show]	artichoke
l'asperge (f.)	[lah-sperj]	asparagus
l'avocat (m.)	[lah-voh-kah]	avocado
la betterave	[lah beht-rahv]	beet, beetroot
la blette	[luh bleht]	chard
le poivron	[luh pwah-vrohn]	bell pepper
le poivron vert	[luh pwah-vrohn vehr]	green bell pepper
le brocoli	[luh broh-koh-lee]	croccoli
le chou	[luh shoo]	cabbage
le chou-fleur	[luh shoo-fler]	cauliflower
le céleri	[luh say-leh-ree]	celery
la chicorée	[lah chee-ko-ray]	chicory
les frites	[lay freet]	chips, French fries, crisps
la carotte	[lah cah-rot]	carrot
le maïs	[luh may-eez]	corn
le concombre	[luh kohn-kohm-br]	cucumber
l'aubergine (f.)	[l'oh-ber-jheen]	eggplant
la scarole	[lah scah-roll]	endive
les petits pois (m.)	[lay puh-tee pwah]	green peas
le chou frisé	[luh shoo free-zay]	kale [a green]
le poireau	[luh pwah-row]	leek
l'oignon (m.)	[loh-nyohn]	onion
le radis	[luh rah-dee]	radish
la ciboule	[lah see-bool]	scallion
l'échalote (f.)	[lay-shaw-lot]	shallot
l'oseille (f.)	[low-say-ya]	sorrel

l'épinard (m.)	[leh-pee-nar]	spinach
la courge	[lah coorj	squash
la tomate	[lah toe-maht]	tomato
la truffe	[lah truhf]	truffle
le navet	[luh nah-vay]	turnip
les legumes (m.)	[lay lay-guhm]	vegetables
le cresson	[luh creh-sohn]	watercress
la courgette	[lah coor-jet]	zucchini

Fish and Seafood (le poisson et les fruits de mer)

la palourde	[lah pah-loord]	clam
le crabe	[luh krahb]	crab
l'écrivisse (m.)	[lay zay-kruh-vees]	crayfish
le carrelet	[luh kahr-leh]	flounder
le flétan	[luh flay-than]	halibut
le hareng	[luh ah-rahN]	herring
le homard	[luh oh-mahr]	lobster
la moule	[lah mool]	mussel
l'huïtre (f.)	[lwee-truh]	oyster
la perche rouge	[lah pehrsh roozh]	red snapper
le saumon	[luh so-mohN]	salmon
la sardine	[lah sahr-deen]	sardine
les coquilles	[lay koh-kee]	scallops
le bar, le loup	[luh bahr, luh loop]	sea bass
la crevette	[lah kruh-veht]	shrimp
l'escargot (m.)	[lehs-kahr-go]	snail
la sole	[lah sohl]	sole
le calmar	[luh kahl-mahr]	squid
l'espadon (m.)	[lehs-pah-dohN]	swordfish
la truite	[lah trweet]	trout
le thon	[luh tohN]	tuna

Grocery Shopping (les courses)

la viande	[lah vyahNd]	meat
la boulangerie	[lah boo-lahNzh-ree]	bakery
les desserts	[lay duh-sehr]	desserts
la charuterie	[lah shahr-keww-tree]	delicatessen
l'épicerie	[lay-pees-ree]	grocery

les légumes (m.)	[lay lay-gewm]	vegetables
les provisions (f.)	[lay proh-vee-zyohN]	provisions
la boucherie	[lah boosh-ree]	butcher shop
viandes froides	[lay vyahNd frwahd]	coldcuts
la confiserie	[lah kohN-feez-ree]	candy store
les bonbons (m.)	[lay bohN-bohN]	candies
la crémerie	[lah kraym-ree]	dairy store
les produits	[leh proh-dwee leh-tyay]	dairy products
la fruiterie	[la frwee-tree]	fruit store
les fruits (m.)	[lay frwee]	fruits
la pâtisserie	[lah pah-tees-ree]	pastry shop, pastry
la poissonnerie	[lah pwah-sohn-ree]	fish store
le poisson	[luh pwah-sohN]	fish
le hypermarché	[luh ee-pehr-mahr-shay]	large supermarket

Countries (les pays)

l'Algérie	[lahl-zhay-ree]	Algeria
l'Allemagne	[lahl-mah-nyuh]	Germany
l'Angleterre	[lahN-gluh-tehr]	England
l'Autriche	[lo-treesh]	Austria
la Belgique	[lah behl-zheek]	Belgium
la Chine	[lah sheen]	China
l'Égypte	[lay-zheept]	Egypt
l'Espagne	[lehs-pah-nyuh]	Spain
la France	[lah frahNs]	France
la Grèce	[lah grehs]	Greece
l'Haïti	[lah-ee-tee]	Haiti
l'Italie	[lee-tah-lee]	Italy
la Pologne	[lah poh-loh-nyuh]	Poland
la Roumanie	[lah roo-mah-nee]	Romania
la Russie	[lah rew-see]	Russia
la Suisse	[lah swees]	Switzerland
la Tunisie	[lah tew-nee-zee]	Tunisia
le Canada	[luh kah-nah-dah]	Canada
le Cambodge	[luh kahN-bohdzh]	Cambodia
les États-Unis	[lay zay-tah-zew-nee]	United States
l'Israël	[leez-rah-ehl]	Israel
le Japon	[luh zhah-pohN]	Japan
le Liban	[luh lee-bahN]	Lebanon
le Maroc	[luh mah-rohk]	Morocco
le Mexique	[luh mehk-seek]	Mexico
la République Démocratique du Congo	[lah reh-poob-leek dem-oh-cra-teek do con-go]	Democratic Republic of Congo

Continents

l'Afrique	[lah-freek]	Africa
l'Amérique du Nord	[lah-may-reek dew nohr]	North America
l'Amérique du Sud	[lah-may-reek dew sewd]	South America
l'Antarctique	[lahn-tahrk-teek]	Antarctica
l'Asie	[lah-zee]	Asia
l'Australie	[loh-strah-lee]	Australia
l'Europe	[lew-rohp]	Europe

Colors (les couleurs)

beige	[behzh]	beige
gris(e)	[gree(z)]	gray
vert(e)	[vehr(t)]	green
noir(e)	[nwahr]	black
bleu(e)	[bluh]	blue
orange	[oh-rahNzh]	orange
brun(e)	[bruhN (brewn)]	brown
rose	[roz]	pink
mauve	[mov]	purple
blanc (he)	[blahN(sh)]	white
rouge	[roozh]	red
jaune	[zhon]	yellow

Parts of the Body (les parties du corps)

la cheville	ankle
l'oeil, les yeux (m.)	eye, eyes
le bras	arm
le sourcil	eyebrow
le dos	back
le cil	eyelash
le ventre	belly
la paupière	eyelid
le cerveau	brain
le doigt	finger
le mollet	calf
l'ongle (m.)	fingernail
la poitrine	chest
le pied	foot
le menton	chin
le front	forehead
l'oreille (f.)	ear
l'esprit (m.)	mind
le coude	elbow
l'estomac (m.)	stomach
la gencive	gum
le nez	nose
les cheveux	hair
la côte	rib
la main	hand
la dent	teeth
la tête	head
la cuisse	thigh
le talon	heel

la gorge	throat
le genou	knee
l'orteil (m.)	toe
la jambe	leg
l'ongle de l'orteil (m.)	toenail
les lèvres (f.)	lips
la langue	tongue
la bouche	mouth
le poignet	wrist
le cou	neck

Family (La famille)

le père	[luh pehr]	father
la mère	[lah mehr]	mother
le grand-père	[luh grahN-pehr]	grandfather
la grand-mère	[lah graN-mehr]	grandmother
le beau-père	[luh bo- pehr]	father-in-law
la belle-mère	[lah behl- mehr]	mother-in-law
l'enfant	[lahN-fahN]	child
le frère	[luh frehr]	brother
la soeur	[lah suhr]	sister
le demi-frère	[luh duh-mee frehr]	step-brother
la demi-soeur	[lah duh-meesuhr]	step-sister
le beau-fils	[luh bo- fees]	step-son, son-in-law
la belle-fille	[lah behl- fee-y]	step-daughter, daughter-in-law
le fils	[luh fees]	son
la fille	[lah fee-y]	daughter
l'oncle	[lohNkl]	uncle
la tante	[lah tahNt]	aunt
le cousin	[luh koo-zahN]	cousin
la cousine	[lah koo-zeen]	cousin
le neveu	[luh nuh-vuh]	nephew
la nièce	[lah nyehs]	niece
le mari	[luh mah-ree]	husband
la femme	[lah fahm]	wife
le gendre	[luh zhahNdr]	son-in-law
le petit ami	[luh puh-tee tahmee]	boyfriend
la petite amie	[lah puh-tee tahmee]	girlfriend

Animals (les animaux)

le léopard	leopard
l'ours (m.)	bear
le lama	llama
le castor	beaver
le singe	monkey
le chat	cat
la souris	mouse
le chimpanzé	chimpanzee
le panda	panda
le cerf	deer
le manchot	penguin
le chien	dog
l'animal domestique (m.)	pet
l'éléphant (m.)	elephant
le chiot	puppy
le poisson	fish
le lapin	rabbit
le renard	fox
le rat	rat
la chèvre	goat
le rhinocéros	rhinoceros
le gorille	gorilla
le mouton	sheep
l'hippopotame (m.)	hippopotamus
l'écureuil (m.)	squirrel
le cheval	horse
le tigre	tiger
l'hyène (f.)	hyena
la baleine	whale

le kangourou	kangaroo
le loup	wolf
le chaton	kitten
le zébra	zebra

School Supplies (les fournitures scolaires)

le sac à dos	backpack
la colle	glue
la serviette	briefcase
le marqueur	marker
la calculatrice	calculator
le porte-mine	mechanical pencil
la chaise	chair
le carnet	notebook
le crayon de couleur	colored pencil
le papier	paper
l'ordinateur (m.)	computer
le stylo	pen
les craies grasses	crayons
le crayon	pencil
le bureau	desk
l'agrafe (f.)	staple
la chemise	folder
l'agrafeuse (f.)	stapler

Occupations (les professions)

le comptable	accountant
le pompier	firefighter
l'acteur (m.)	actor
le coiffeur	hair dresser
l'artiste (f.)	artist
le juge	judge
l'athlète (f.)	athlete
l'avocat (m.)	lawyer, attorney
le coiffeur	barber
le bibliothécaire	librarian
le patron	boss
le facteur	mailman, postman
l'homme d'affaires (m.)	businessman
le maçon	mason, brick layer
le boucher	butcher
le mécanicien	mechanic
le menuisier	carpenter
l'infirmière (f.)	nurse
le caissier	cashier
le policier	police officer
le chef	chef
le président	president
l'entraîneur (m.)	coach
le professeur (m.)	professor, teacher
le technicien informatique	computer technician
le programmeur	programmer
l'ouvrier (m.)	construction worker
le journaliste	reporter

le dentiste	dentist
le secrétaire	secretary
le médecin	doctor
le vétérinaire	veterinarian
l'ingénieur	engineer
le serveur	waiter
le fermier	farmer
l'écrivain (m.)	writer

Sports (les sports)

le badminton	badminton
le hockey	hockey
le base-ball	baseball
l'équitation	horseback riding
le basket	basketball
le ping-pong	ping pong
le cricket	cricket
le rugby	rugby
le cyclisme	cycling
le foot	soccer
le football américain	football
la notation	swimming
le match	game, match (sporting event)
l'équipe	team
le golf	golf
le tennis	tennis
le handball	handball
le volley	volleyball

Car Parts (les pieces de voiture)

la transmission automatique	automatic transmission
la transmission	manual transmission
l'essieu (m.)	axle
le rétroviseur	rearview mirror
les freins (m.)	brakes
la ceinture de sécurité	seat belt
le pare-chocs	bumper
le pneu de rechange	spare tire
le conducteur	driver
le volant	steering wheel
le moteur	engine
le toit vitré	sun roof
la première	first gear
le feu arrière	taillight
l'essence (f.)	gas, petrol
le pneu	tire
l'accélérateur (m.)	gas pedal
le coffre	trunk
le réservoir à essence	gas tank
le feu de direction	turn signal
le levier de vitesses	gear shift
la visière	visor
les phares (m.)	headlights
la roue	wheel
la capote	hood
la vitre	window
le klaxon	horn
le pare-brise	windshield

le cric	jack
l'essuie-glace (m.)	wipers

Nature (la nature)

l'escarpement	cliff
l'océan	ocean
la fleur	flower
la plante	the plant
la cour	yard
le fleuve, la rivière	river
le jardin	garden, orchard
la mer	sea
la pelouse	grass (lawn)
la plage, le bord de la mer	shore
l'herbe (f.)	herb
le sol	soil
le lac	lake
l'arbre (m.)	tree
la chaîne de montagnes	mountain range
la cascade	waterfall
la montagne	mountain
la mauvaise herbe	weed

Appliances (les appareils)

le mixeur	blender
le micro-onde	microwave
le lave-vaisselle	dishwasher
le four	oven
le séchoir	dryer
le grille-pain	toaster
le congélateur	freezer
la machine à laver	washer
le chauffe-eau	water heater
le réfrigérateur	fridge
le fer à repasser	iron

The Bedroom (la chambre)

le réveil	alarm clock
le cintre	hanger
le lit	bed
la lampe	lamp
la table de nuit	nightstand
la couverture	blanket
l'oreiller (m.)	pillow
le plafond	ceiling
les draps	sheets
la penderie	closet
le mur	wall
la commode	dresser

Tools (les outils)

la hache	axe
les pinces	pliers
l'essieu (m.)	axle
la poulie	pulley
la barre	bar
la rampe	ramp
la lame	blade
la corde	rope, cord
la règle	ruler
la perceuse	drill
la scie	saw
la mèche	drill bit
le tournevis	screwdriver
la lampe de poche	flashlight
le mètre enrouleur	tape measure
le marteau	hammer
le manche	handle
la roue	wheel
le couteau	knife
le tourne-à-gauche	wrench
l'écrou (m.)	nut (as in nut and bolt)

16371944R00075

Printed in Poland
by Amazon Fulfillment
Poland Sp. z o.o., Wrocław